W9-BAT-779

"Fr. Ken's work in making the Psalms more accessible to recovering people is amazing. His understanding of Scripture and the nuances of recovering people is very evident throughout this book. Guest House will incorporate this book into our curriculum."

— Jeff Henrich, President and CEO
Guest House, Inc., Michigan

"This work speaks profoundly to me as a recovering person. Ken has captured the very spirit of the Twelve Steps, facilitating one to personalize God as he understands him. This book would be an inspirational addition to daily prayer and meditation."

— Terry Brown
Kalamazoo, Michigan

"This adaptation of the Psalms to a language that is universal to all who experience addiction is refreshing and unique. Kenneth Schmidt captures the heart of prayer in this beautiful translation. The introduction is particularly useful in orienting people to the benevolence of God's love and provides a segue into the body of the Psalms with an orientation to the essence of the 3rd and 11th steps. A remarkable work!"

— LuAngela Cervone
Kalamazoo, Michigan

"Fr. Ken has captured the essence of the Psalms as well as the essence of the 12-step recovery vernacular. His poetry grasps the spiritual depths of the despair that comes in addiction, the hope and eventual gratitude and praise that can be offered in recovery. I recommend this book as a tool for anyone who is comfortable with the biblical foundation as they grapple with the pain of addiction, the challenges, and the joys of recovery."

— Rev. Dr. Deborah Kohler, 37 years in recovery
Portage, Michigan

"'Listen God, I've got a problem . . .' (Psalm 17) is just one of many prayers Father Ken has transformed for an addict, or anyone wishing to pray the Psalms in present day. This contemporary version of sacred songs and lamentations is graceful and truthful; really resonating with those desiring to grow closer to God. Truly inspiring!"

— Colleen Semler
Kalamazoo, Michigan

"Ken has grasped the core message of each Psalm. He has then splashed on these pages: my thoughts, my struggles, my experience and my joy, in my 12-step language. My relationship with God has once again been deepened."

— Kathy Davies
Portage, Michigan

Conscious Contact with God

The Psalms for Addiction and Recovery

Kenneth W. Schmidt

LITURGICAL PRESS
Collegeville, Minnesota

www.litpress.org

Cover design by Monica Bokinskie. Photo courtesy of Getty images.

© 2019 by Kenneth W. Schmidt
Published by Liturgical Press, Collegeville, Minnesota. All rights
reserved. No part of this book may be used or reproduced in any
manner whatsoever, except brief quotations in reviews, without
written permission of Liturgical Press, Saint John's Abbey,
PO Box 7500, Collegeville, MN 56321-7500. Printed in the United
States of America.

1　　2　　3　　4　　5　　6　　7　　8　　9

Library of Congress Cataloging-in-Publication Data

Names: Schmidt, Kenneth W., author.
Title: Conscious contact with God: psalms for addiction and recovery
　/ Kenneth W. Schmidt.
Description: Collegeville : Liturgical Press, 2019. | Summary: "A new
　paraphrase of the Psalms that reflects the experience of addiction
　and living in recovery"—Provided by publisher.
Identifiers: LCCN 2019003108 (print) | LCCN 2019981081 (ebook) |
　ISBN 9780814664155 (pbk.) | ISBN 9780814664407 (ebook)
Subjects: LCSH: Bible. Psalms—Paraphrases, English. | Twelve-step
　programs—Religious aspects—Christianity.
Classification: LCC BS1440 .S3337 2019 (print) | LCC BS1440 (ebook)
　| DDC 223/.205209--dc23
LC record available at https://lccn.loc.gov/2019003108
LC ebook record available at https://lccn.loc.gov/2019981081

Contents

Preface

People experience addiction in many ways. Some are addicted to a substance, such as alcohol or heroin. Others are addicted to a behavior, such as gambling or masturbation. Others experience their addiction in a more general way but it may be just as compulsive and debilitating, such as work or overeating. In these psalms I have used an *X* in the text, so that the reader/pray-er can substitute his or her own specific addictive substance or behavior.

These paraphrased psalms are based on an English translation in the public domain called the *World English Bible*. While I often follow the text, there are occasions when there is not a close alignment between the *WEB* and my paraphrase. In some cases the English original is an inspiration or "jumping-off point" for the paraphrased version that expresses the viewpoint of someone with an addiction who is going through recovery and following the Twelve Steps.

For example, Psalms 104 and 106 substitute a description of the Steps in place of extended accounts of creation and Jewish salvation history. Psalm 119 is extremely repetitious because it uses eight different terms for the Law in each of twenty-two sections. So in this book I follow the psalm's convention of all the stanzas in each section starting with the same letter of the Hebrew alphabet, and instead include a collection of Twelve-Step truisms for each letter of the English alphabet that provides the reader/pray-er a rich source of material for meditation.

I chose to change the psalms in most places to the voice of first person (the reader) addressed to second person (God, Higher Power) to make them more clearly prayers, in order to speak directly to God and not "about God." I tried to avoid gendered pronouns in reference to God. I also tried to maintain some of the rhythm and alliteration of the poetry while writing this paraphrased text, with more success in some psalms than others.

Introduction

Addiction, Recovery, and Prayer

In Twelve-Step programs, Step 11 says that we "sought through prayer and meditation to improve our conscious contact with God *as we understood [God]*, praying only for knowledge of [God's] will for us and the power to carry that out." That's easier said than done, whether it's people recovering from addictions or anyone else.

There seem to be four components of this Step:

* prayer and meditation;

* conscious contact with God;

* knowledge of God's will for us;

* power to carry it out.

The first component describes the means to be used, i.e., prayer and meditation. The next three components describe the goals: to be in touch with God; to discern what God wants; and to have the power to do it. After all, what good is it to *know* God's will if we don't try to *act* on it? (James 1:22-25; 2:14-17.)

For a good number of people, including those recovering from addictions, there is discomfort with the idea of prayer. They may be able to do no more than read from a book of prayers that others have written. Others may only know about a few styles or ways of praying, and are not acquainted with the rich variety of prayer styles throughout human history. They also may believe they "don't pray" because their style does not correspond to what they were taught. Or they don't "pray well" because of their discomfort, which is related to a mismatch between their personality or temperament and the prayer style they use.

Attempts to pray can be hampered, then, by the beliefs or knowledge that people have about prayer. If they believe that prayer is "talking to God," then they miss out on the mutual relationship of prayer. If they believe that prayer is only done by really holy people, then they may not try to pray because of a misplaced sense of humility.

Some people have little or no expectation that their prayer will open them to a personal encounter with God. It is performed because of a sense of obedience or duty. They don't think they will *hear* or *experience* God in their prayer, and if something does happen, they distrust it.

Attempts to pray can also be impeded by people's beliefs about God *as they understand God*. Their image of God as a harsh judge may stoke their fear; and an image of God as father may adversely affect the prayer of those who were abused by their fathers. One author compiled a list of more than one hundred biblical names for God! Shepherd, Servant, Rock, Refuge, Light, Life, Morning Star, Bread of Life—each of them can open people to new understandings and ways to encounter God, and broaden *how they understand God*.

Therefore, Step 11 is difficult for many people, and may even provoke resistance. They don't want to pray; they don't know, or believe, or trust God; or they don't know how to pray or what to say.

A good place to start is the book of Psalms in the Old Testament of the Bible. It is a collection of prayer-songs compiled over a period of several hundred years, and used by Jews and Christians for over twenty-five hundred years. Sometimes the collection even has been called a "school for prayer." The Psalms include beautiful words of praise for God; laments or expressions of grief; petitions for God's assistance; confessions of weakness and sin; and words of profound gratitude.

[margin note: kinds of Psalms]

There are some frequent themes in the psalms, and those who know addiction and recovery can easily relate to them. Experiences of being in the depths, crying out for help, and being the scorn of neighbors might not be a common experience for many people, but they are well known by people suffering with addictions. Seeking a refuge and being saved might not speak immediately to middle-class Americans, but they speak loudly to people who have suffered and to those who are in recovery. Gratitude to God because they are alive and have not been lost to the enemy (addiction) is real.

[margin note: Themes in Psalms]

The Psalms also are a school for prayer because they help people learn how to pray. When the words of a psalm aren't sufficient, they can begin to express their own heartfelt fear, sadness, and awe, their appeals, and their thanksgiving. They do not have to be tied to a text written by someone else.

[margin note: (A]

Finally, the Psalms are a school for prayer because they help those who pray to know God and to know themselves better. In the end, prayer does not have the power to change God. Saying the right words or repeating them enough times does not wear God down or change God's mind. But the school of prayer may slowly mold their thinking, feeling, and believing to understand who God really is and to let go of the false or warped image of God that they have.

[margin note: (B]

Over time, they may discover that God is not disappointed in them, or burdened by them. In fact, the psalms tell us that God delights in them, a far cry from the shame that many people feel.

In prayer they will discover that God has already initiated a relationship because God precedes them, and God always acts first—they can offer no more than a response. God has already demonstrated the desire to heal them and fill them. They will meet God who is able to live with their contradictions; God who is able to love people with their ambiguity; God who loves those who themselves are both weeds and wheat.

From the divine perspective, God does not want a one-sided relationship, although God may show an immense amount of patience in waiting for people to respond. Nor does God want a relationship that from the human perspective is founded on fear, or obedience, or even a divine imperative to love God. God is inviting a mutual relationship, an intimate bond in which "my Beloved is mine, and I belong to my Beloved" (Song of Songs 2:16).

May these psalms help you find God and fall in love, and thus be healed.

PSALM 1

Happy are we who do not follow
the insanity of our addiction,
nor walk the path of our disease,
nor hang out with those "who have no problem."
Rather in the Twelve Steps we find joy, *in the Law of the LORD*
and we <u>study</u> these Steps carefully. *meditate on day & night*
We become like trees
planted near flowing streams
that grow bountifully *yields its fruit in due seaso*
and help others to find sobriety. *- the Bodhisatva*
We do not succumb in the face of temptation;
surprisingly, we now prosper.
But that's not always the case for fellow addicts.
They can be like mown grass tossed about by the wind.
They may not survive the course of their disease,
and may even drag others down with them.
God provides all addicts a path to recovery
but some choose to stay on the path to death.

PSALM 2

Why do so many of us protest
and grumble against God?
Why has God done this to me?
Why has God afflicted me?
God has never done anything for me.
I have no need for God!"
And so God laughs

and hoots from heaven.
God speaks with authority
and causes us to fall down in awe:
"I myself will lift you up
and set you on the throne of recovery.
I will provide the Steps for your healing,
for you are a beloved child to me.
You have only to ask,
and I will free you from your disease
and give you the fullness of sobriety.
You will find the sure path to recovery
and your harmful cravings will be destroyed."
So now, all addicts, listen up!
Pay attention to what God offers us:
"Hand over your life to me
and follow the Steps religiously
or else you will die
because of your insanity."
We who put our trust in God are saved!

PSALM 3

1) I have so many cravings, God!   *foes*   Oh Lord, how many are my foes
Temptations come at me from every direction!   *foes*   Many are rising, against me
2) *"Foes"* Family and friends say   *foes*
I cannot be saved.   "There is no help for you in God
3) But God, you are my strength
and you help me hold my head high.
4) Whenever I cry out to you for help,

"he answers"

you <u>will</u> always answer my prayer.

5) I trust that even as I go to sleep

you will cause me to rise the next morning.

6) So I am not afraid of my <u>intense desires</u> *"tens of thousands of people"*

that surround me on every side.

7) Come to me, God! Save me, Higher Power!

"you strike" *all my enemies*

Destroy <u>the crazy thoughts that arise</u> (within) me.

Smash my relentless temptations.

8) For my sobriety only comes from you. *"Deliverance belongs to the Lord"*

PSALM 4

Heb: "righteousness"

1) When I call, answer me, God of <u>healing.</u> — *"of my right!"*

Heb: "You From my addiction <u>you released me;</u> — *"you gave me room, when I was in distress"*

Make a wideness for me in a narrow space"

2) How long will the addicted mock you,

crave what is poison, and swallow their own lies?

3) I know that you, Higher Power, work wonders,

and hear me when I cry out for help.

4) I am in awe of what you have done;

I recall each night your gift of my abstinence.

5) Sobriety is my goal, one day at a time,

and I place my trust in you.

6) Some ask, "What can bring us relief?"

God, you are the answer to my prayers.

7) You have given me more joy

than others have from their possessions and wealth.

8) And so I lie down in peace to sleep,

knowing that you are the one who keeps me safe.

PSALM 5

1) Listen, to me, God!

Listen as I groan.

2) Hear my cry for help again,

Higher Power, God!

I pray to you, God,

3) that this morning you will hear me.

This morning I pray once more,

watching and waiting,

while the arrogant have no need of you.

4) For you do not delight in <u>my addiction,</u> *"wickedness"*

and you find no pleasure in my disease.

5) You hate all illness

and want to destroy all false desires.

6) You want to quash <u>all cravings</u> *"those who speak lies"*

and <u>unhealthy temptations.</u> *"bloodthirsty and deceitful"*

7) But through the greatness of your love

I have been given sobriety!

Today I am clean and abstinent   *"bow down toward your*

only because of you.   *Holy Temple because of you."*

8) Guide me <u>on this path of healing</u> *"in your righteousness"*

and <u>clear the path to keep me clean.</u> *"make your way straight before me"*

Protect me today from the insanity

of those who deceive themselves.

9) Their words are a path to the grave

although they sound sweet to my ears.

10) Help them see their own disease,

to recognize the depth of their illness.

Push aside their faults and failures
that come from ignoring you.
11) I have found sobriety by finding you
and so I cry out with joy.
Protect me from myself;
protect all who count on your power.
12) For you indeed <u>rescue the addicted</u>, ("*bless the righteous*")
Heb.
and surround us with saving power.

PSALM 6

Do not scold me, God,
or punish me in your anger.
Show me mercy,
because I am exhausted.
Heal me,
because my body is worn out,
and my mind is filled with pain.
How long, God, before you act?
Turn to me; save me!
Rescue me from this hellish life.
For if I'm dead, I cannot pray,
and I certainly can't praise you
while I'm in this living hell.
I'm tired of complaining about my life;
my bed is wet from my sobbing.
My eyes are red from my crying
and swollen from all my tears.
Get away from me, you awful cravings!

My Higher Power has heard me.
God has seen my weeping
and paid heed to my cries.
My crazy thoughts and unhealthy desires
will be cast aside by God's power.

PSALM 7

God, I appeal to you for help.
Save me from this terrible illness
that's tearing apart my life
and destroys everything I've tried to do.
God, if I have done anything wrong,
if I have returned evil deeds for good things done for me,
then I now confess these wrongs.
Make me ready to face the truth
and to accept the consequences.
I'm ready for you to remove my character defects.
Come to me, God, in all your strength,
and take away my shortcomings.
You know better than I what needs your healing.
Let me know those whom I have harmed.
Make out the list; show me their names;
give me the willingness to make amends to them all.
Restore my life as I make just amends;
free me from the burden of lifelong guilt;
rescue me from the crushing weight of shame.
You will protect me as I seek the truth,
and let me feel the sting of my deception.

You will give me the awareness to admit my wrongdoing,

and let me feel the pain that I have caused others.

For we addicts produce pain

and freely spread it around.

We dig holes we cannot escape;

we fall into them and cannot get out.

Our actions circle 'round and bite us in the butt,

for what goes 'round comes back on us again.

I thank you, God, for your healing;

I celebrate the might of my Higher Power.

PSALM 8   *Superscription is gone!*

1 God, you are awesome!

Your greatness is proclaimed around the world. *"your Glory above Heavens (Heb: NRSV?)*

2 Young and old speak of your miracles, *(enemy : avenger)*

because you have conquered our addictions;

this makes others shut their critical mouths.

3 When I consider the universe, filled with celestial bodies,

the galaxies spread through the heavens,

4 then what is a human being, *(s) – in NRSV : Heb*

a mere lump of mortal flesh,

that you would care so much for me?

5 Yet you made me *(them)* just a little less than you,

gilding me with beauty and goodness.

6 You entrusted me *(them)* with care for your creation,

made me *(them)* responsible to care for my home:

7 Everything you made—abundant food and water,

flocks in the field and beasts of the jungle,

8   and all that fills the skies and the seas.
9   God, you are awesome!

PSALM 9

I am grateful to you, my God,
and will thank you for your great deeds.
I will acclaim you each day
and will praise your power forever.
When addiction arose in my life,
it fell to the ground before your might.
You fight for my sobriety,
and offer the Steps that can save me.
You rescue me from stupidity,
and save me from impulsivity.
You free me from my deceptions
and help me to recognize your truth.
Your healing endures for the ages;
you offer the Steps that can save me.
You show the way to sobriety,   *"the way..."*
and guide me on the path to clean living.
Your power energizes the oppressed,
and is strength for those addicted.
When we know you as you are,
we place our trust in you,
for you never abandon us to our disease.
We give thanks to you in our groups,
and tell of your healing at our meetings,
for you hear the cries of our suffering,

and never forget the anguish of the addicted.

Be kind to me, Higher Power;

see the pain beneath my compulsion.

You are the only one who can save me,

so that I can sing your praises

and speak of your deliverance

within the recovering community.

So many have succumbed to their addiction;

they cannot hide how far they have fallen.

You have revealed your power to us

who are burdened by this awful disease.

They may remain trapped by its weight,

and never look up to see you, God.

Those in pain won't be overlooked,

and the oppressed will never be forgotten.

Come to us, God;

don't let our addictions prevail;

conquer the disease among us.

Come, Higher Power; drive it away,

for we're only human,

and can't do it on our own.

PSALM 10

God, why do you keep your distance?

Why do you hide yourself when I'm in trouble?

My addiction persecutes me,

and I'm caught in its terrible grip.

This disease has corrupted my heart's desires;

it's greedy for things which damage my soul.

Others believe that there is no one to save me;

I've begun to believe that there is no God.

In addiction we think we'll never prosper;

we believe our recovery is impossible.

Or we deny that we have a problem,

that this disease could never drag *us* down.

Our minds are filled with anger and fear,

and our mouths with deception and lies.

Our disease waits to trip us up;

it hides in wait for another day.

The illness watches for my weakness,

it lies in wait like an animal of prey.

It hides itself; it's ready to pounce,

to seize my soul and drag me away.

We're innocent addicts who bob and weave;

we're helpless, and get knocked to the ground.

We believe in our hearts we're forgotten,

that God will never see our destruction.

Get up, God! Fight for us!

Do not abandon us now.

Don't let the disease be the winner;

or let us think that it's stronger than you.

You do see!

You take note of our troubles

and join in the fight.

As the powerless we turn to you;

you are the help of the innocent.

Knock it down; break its bones;

destroy the addiction that's beating me.

You are our Higher Power,

our God who can banish this disease.

God, you hear the cry of the humble,

those who know they can't do it alone.

You bring your healing to the oppressed,

so that addiction no longer has power.

PSALM 11

In you, God, I place my trust.

How can they suggest that I run away?

My addiction will always be with me,

no matter where I go.

If I don't rely on my Higher Power

I will never recover.

You are in the heavens;

from there you behold my plight.

Your loving gaze beholds me.

You probe the human heart;

you abhor my suffering.

You destroy the disease that afflicts me;

you blow it away as your gift to me.

For you are always good,

and always desire what is good for me.

One day I shall behold you, too.

PSALM 12

1 Help me, Higher Power,
   for no one else can do it.
2 My sobriety has gone down the tubes.
   I tell more lies to cover my shame;
   I hide my failure with doublespeak.
3 Save me, God, from my deceitful tongue,   — *boasting*
   from the dishonesty that leads me to X;
4 I convince myself that X will help me,
   I have no one to blame but myself.
5 You tell me, "I will come to you;
   you need me, and I will save you.
   I will give you the peace you long for."
6 Your promises, my God, are trustworthy;
   your word is dependable,
   and your assurances will be honored.
7 You will protect us in our helplessness;
   you will save us from our addictions,
8 though temptation is all around us.
   Its false promises haunt humankind.

PSALM 13

My God, how long will it be?
Will you forget me forever?
How long will you hide from me?
How long must I bear this pain?
How long will I carry this sorrow?
How long will this addiction weigh me down?

Think on me and give me your answer;

send your light or I'll succumb to the darkness.

The addiction will be victorious

and I'll die a hundred deaths.

I put my trust in your saving love;

my heart will rejoice as you save me.

I will raise my voice in song,

because you've been good to me.

PSALM 14

1 Only fools say, "There is no God."

They deceive themselves with their power;

they think they can save themselves.

2 You look down upon us from heaven,

ready to respond to the wise,

to all who seek your help.

3 Those who continue to X,

they do not believe.

"have gone aside"

They have no need for you.

Soon they'll succumb to their fear,

while you will rescue believers.

Deliverance will come from you, God.

Our Higher Power will restore us,

and we'll be filled with joy and gladness.

PSALM 15

God, who can know you?

Who can discover you, Higher Power?

Those who surrender to you;
those who seek your will
and the power to carry it out;
who do not deceive themselves
or cause harm to others;
who promptly admit their wrongs,
and are willing to make amends;
who practice the Twelve Steps,
and carry the message to others.
Those who do these things
will stay strong in their sobriety.

PSALM 16

Protect me, God,
because I take my refuge in you.
I say, "You are my Higher Power;
there is no sobriety without you."
We who enjoy recovery are blessed,
you find great delight in us.
But we who choose another god,
who in crisis turn to X,
just make things worse for ourselves
and heap suffering on those we love.
Knowing you is the best reward;
you hold my fate in your hands.
You've brought me to a good place
just as you have promised.
I am grateful for your wisdom;

even in the night you give me counsel.

I keep you always in my sight,

with you at my side I will not succumb.

My heart is glad, my being rejoices;

my body is at peace.

For you never give up on me,

and won't let the "bottom" be the end.

You show me the path to life;

with you there is a full life,

and satisfaction that endures.

PSALM 17

Listen, God, I've got a problem;

Let me make my case the best I can.

Please fix me and make things right.

If you look into my heart,

even catch me by surprise,

you know that I'm not wicked,

and I don't intend to deceive.

I've done my best to be truthful

and not to cause others pain.

I'm trying to follow the Steps

and not fall off the wagon.

I ask for your help; answer me.

Listen to me, and respond to my need.

Manifest your great power,

you who offer refuge,

and save me from this dread disease.

Show me your special favor;

give me shelter under your care.

Save me from deadly dependence;

protect me from compulsive behaviors.

The cravings show no compassion;

they don't care who's harmed in the process.

They track me down and find me;

they discover my weak spots and attack.

They prowl like wild beasts,

ready to harass me again.

Rise up, God, and conquer them;

drive them out and set me free.

Save me from all who seek my life,

who only think of themselves.

What they offer is no good for me;

it lasts a bit and then fades away;

nothing satisfies as much as I'd hoped.

In the morning I will rise from sleep

and know that you are with me.

PSALM 18

I love you, God, my strength,

The one in whom I find shelter.

You are my rock; my fortress; deliverance;

my stronghold; my safety; salvation.

I call out to you, Higher Power,

and thus I am saved from addiction.

I was ensnared in the ropes of death;

the floods of doom surged over me;
the flames of damnation lapped at me;
the pit of death stared up at me.
In distress I cried out to you;
I begged for your help.
You heard my desperation;
you listened to my plea.
The ground shook on which I stood;
things changed as you entered my life.
You were roused to come to my rescue;
you left your high heavens to save me.
Your power was unleashed in my mind;
my body was renewed by your strength.
You broke through clouds of confusion
and the darkness that filled my soul.
You spoke a word of healing,
as strong as "Let there be light."
Your truth set fire to my lies;
your honesty burned in my heart.
You cut to the chase, yes, you did;
you laid bare my life's depravity.
You reached out and pulled me up;
you rescued me when I was drowning.
You delivered me from my addiction,
which tried to destroy my life;
it was too strong for me.
It started as a day of calamity,
and concluded with your support.

You brought me to a safe place
because you delight in me. Go figure!
Now you reward me for my goodness,
and bless me for my integrity.
Now I seek your will and follow your path,
and turn away from my false gods.
I follow the Steps and Traditions,
and do not fall down in shame.
I admit my wrongdoing
and acknowledge my defects.
Now you reward me for my goodness,
in accordance with my integrity.
As we are faithful, so are you;
as we live without blame, so do you.
You respond to our goodness;
and likewise, to our evil.
You walk alongside the humble,
but the arrogant are way out front.
It is your light that guides me;
your light shines in my darkness.
With your strength, I can climb mountains;
I can scale cliffs with you at my side.
God, you are perfect!
What you say is always true.
You're a shelter for all who seek safety.
For what Power is higher than you?
What rock is stronger than you?
You clothed me with strength

and made my way safe.
I'm secure on the side of a mountain;
I can defend myself when I must.
You provide me with needed armor
to protect myself when tempted.
This is no narrow path I walk;
it's a broad valley of freedom.
I set out to find a new life;
I won't give up 'til I have it.
I examined each fear and resentment;
I considered my ambitions and pride.
You gave me security and friends,
safety and self-esteem.
Negativity struggled to survive;
dishonesty reared its head.
But you beat them back
and destroyed their hold on my life.
Arguments disappeared,
and relationships blossomed.
I grew in consideration,
and accepted help from others.
My words are accepted as truthful;
some can hear my wisdom.
Sponsors take me further,
and I, in turn, teach others.
God lives! My rock is strong.
My Higher Power is praiseworthy.
You gave me victory over X,

and subdued its deadly power.
You delivered me from my addiction,
and raised me from my disease.
So I honor you among the people,
and I sing your praises in public.
You have triumphed over my enemy,
and shown your faithful love
to your child and my descendants forever.

PSALM 19

The earth is filled with God's greatness;
it declares the good news of God's healing.
From day to day the word goes out;
from night to night the message is made known.
Even without words it's clear
that God has accomplished a miracle.
The whole world hears what God has done;
the message has reached the ends of the earth.
We addicts can count on our God
as we've learned to count on the sun.
We know its rising and setting,
its passage from east to west.
It emerges, then disappears;
it's there, and gone, and returns.
The wisdom of God is perfect,
it refreshes my life at its core.
The Steps of the Program are true;
they enliven my mind and my heart.

The principles are just and right;
they bring joy to my life.
The teaching of Twelve Steps is true;
their truth will last forever.
I trust my Higher Power,
whose guidance is certain and firm.
What I receive is better than X,
better than ten times X;
greater than its false promises,
lasting longer than anything else.
We share this message with others—
there's a way out of the depths.
There's something more than what they've heard,
a better life than what they've known.
I won't listen to the deceitful,
nor to the lies of my addiction.
Keep me safe from harmful compulsions,
and innocent of yielding to temptations.
May my words and my actions
be acceptable to you,
my Higher Power who saves me.

PSALM 20

My God, help me in my troubles.
My Higher Power, protect me.
My God, come down from on high
and give me the support I need.
My God, remember my goodness,

and act hastily in my favor.

My God, grant my deepest desire,

and fulfill every one of my hopes.

Soon may I rejoice in my recovery,

and raise a flag to proclaim my victory.

My God, do what I request.

I know you help the chosen,

those selected to be your own,

with a victory won by your great strength.

Some take pride in their cars, and others their homes,

but our pride comes from our Higher Power.

Others may collapse and fall to the earth,

but we will rise up and stand tall.

Give victory to us addicts, God;

hear us and answer our prayer.

PSALM 21

We addicts rejoice in your strength;

we praise the might of our Higher Power.

You have granted us our deepest desire,

and not held back from our request.

You have crowned us with many blessings;

you have granted our greatest wish.

We asked you to save our lives, and you did;

we are still alive to tell the story.

Your greatness is known because you healed us;

we are remarked on because of your gifts.

You do not withhold your blessings;

we are gladdened by your goodness.

We have surrendered to you, great God;

our Higher Power is unwavering in love.

You have searched out our enemies,

the foes who sought to take our lives.

You expunge the addictions from our minds;

you set free our bodies' weaknesses;

you conquer the compulsions that drive us;

you overwhelm the impulses that push us.

You destroy the cravings that fill us,

the temptations that relentlessly taunt.

If we have thoughts of X,

we know they won't prevail,

for you will give us the grace we need

at the moment we need it most.

Be praised, Higher Power!

We sing and praise your might.

PSALM 22

God!

My God!

Why have you abandoned me?

Why have you kept your distance?

Why don't you hear my groans?

I call out in the day, and you do not answer;

I cry out in the night when I cannot sleep.

You are said to be a Higher Power,

stronger than anything else in my life.

Others have placed their trust in you,
and you delivered them from their disease.
They cried out to you, and you saved them;
they trusted you, and you healed them.
But I am unworthy, lower than a snake,
scorned by some, and mocked by others.
They see what I do and despise me;
they insult me and make fun of me.
My friends do otherwise; they urge me,
"Surrender your life to God.
A Higher Power can save you."
You have known me since I was born;
even in the womb you watched over me.
You have held me in tenderness since my birth;
from that day until now you've been my God.
So do not keep your distance
for I'm in a lot of trouble
and there's no one else who can help.
A horrible disease dwells in me;
it fills every corner of my life.
It is tearing apart my life
and destroys everything I try to do.
My life is seeping out,
my bones are turning soft;
my heart is slowing down,
soon it will simply wear out;
my strength is depleted,
my energy used up;

I have nothing left to give.

Temptations come from all 'round me,

the cravings are relentless and strong.

My life is shriveled up;

my body is marked by bruising.

People stare when they see me—

they wonder when I will die

and plan how to split my assets.

Draw near to me, Higher Power!

Come close or I shall die!

Deliver me from my addiction;

save me from this dread disease;

rescue me from the jaws of death.

You have pulled me out of hell.

I will tell my family what you have done,

the assembly of believers will hear my good news.

Those who know a Higher Power, give praise.

May all who have religion glorify you;

and all people of faith give praise.

For you did not stand back in loathing

and leave me to my suffering.

You did not hide in horror,

but heard my cry and saved me.

I remember my pledge to you

and so I praise you in public;

others will learn of your great power

as I testify to your mighty deeds.

The world will learn what you can do

and surrender their lives to you;

my family will rejoice in my recovery

and come to you with thanksgiving.

For you are the Higher Power,

the one who reigns supreme.

Even those who died should praise you!

They too have learned of your great might

for death has no grip on them.

My descendants will also praise you;

generations to come will know your strength

because of what you've done for me.

PSALM 23

1 God, you're a shepherd for me;   *YHWH 3dP*

now I lack for nothing.

2 You guide me to safe places   *YHWH 3dP*

and lead me to serenity.

3 You restore my life

and keep me on the right path.

4 Even in my darkest times

I am not afraid,

because you are with me;

your presence comforts me.

5 You set a banquet for me

that makes some others jealous.

You anoint me with your spirit,

so I overflow with goodness.

6 Yes, goodness and mercy will fill me   *YHWH 3dP*

every single day of my life.
I will abide in your loving presence
today and my whole life long.

PSALM 24

1 The world belongs to you,
and everything that's in it.
2 You gave us the earth, and skies,
the oceans, and all that fills them.
3 Who can climb that high mountain
and attain the summit of sobriety?
We who follow the Twelve Steps,
who do not listen to falsehoods
and the deceptions of our disease.
We will receive your blessing,
and recovery from our addiction.
We'll gather with those who've been saved,
who have surrendered our lives to you.
Swing wide, you city gates,
open wide, you castle doors,
that our Higher Power may enter!
Who is our Higher Power?
God who is strong and mighty,
God who can heal our disease.
Crumble before him, ancient walls,
Turn to dust, what seeks to exclude,
that our Higher Power may enter!
Who is our Higher Power?

The God who heals us;

that is our Higher Power.

PSALM 25

I surrender my life to you, my God;

I put my wholehearted trust in you.

Don't let this lead to my shame;

don't let my addiction reign.

Don't let those who trust you fail;

rather, let those who avoid you be ashamed.

Help me find the right path, my God;

teach me the Steps.

Lead me on a journey of faith,

for you are the Power who rescues me;

long have I awaited your help.

Remember to show mercy, God,

and remain faithful to your love

as you have done for generations.

Don't remember the sins of my past

nor the resentments I have held against you.

Remember the person whom you created;

for the sake of your goodness, remember.

God shows the way that is good;

my Power leads me through the Steps.

God shows me the path of humility,

and I learn to accept myself.

God leads me on the path of sobriety,

and all who work the Twelve Steps.

I ask you, Higher Power,

to remove my character defects.

We are the ones who recover:

we make amends to those we've harmed.

We will live in serenity,

and our children will grow up in peace.

God's friendship is here for those who listen,

who pay attention to what God has to say.

I pray for knowledge of God's will

and the power to carry it out.

Turn to me and give me your grace,

for I am lost and afflicted.

Allay the troubles of my life,

and save me from my anguish.

Look at me in my distress,

and save me from my guilt.

Consider the strength of my cravings,

and their relentless attacks on my life.

Guard my life, and deliver me,

protect me from all shame,

as I seek my refuge in you.

Let integrity and sobriety save me;

I wait for you and your help.

Rescue your child, O God,

from all my troubles.

PSALM 26

1 You uphold me, Higher Power,

as I strive to walk with integrity,

to trust you one day at a time.

2 Put me to the test, God;

probe my mind and heart.

3 I recall your loving-kindness,

and I remain faithful to the Steps.

walked in your truth

4 I cannot sit with those who use,

or spend time with those who X.

deceitful men hypocrites

It's dangerous to be with those who X,

and I must avoid the people who use.

I do what I can to stay sober,

to stay close to my Higher Power.

I am grateful for your healing power,

for restoring me to sanity.

I enjoy my time of abstinence;

I am grateful for my sobriety.

Don't let me fall off the wagon,

nor succumb to my temptations.

Keep me a safe distance from my cravings,

and preserve my life from my longings.

You uphold me, God, in integrity,

you show mercy to me and redeem me.

Now I am firmly grounded

and speak at meetings about you.

PSALM 27

You give me life, and salvation;
so whom should I fear?
You are the strength of my life;
so what can make me afraid?
When my addictions attack me
and try to seize my life,
my desires and dependencies
stumble and fall to the ground.
Even if many compulsions arise,
my heart will not fear;
even if my disease declares war,
I will remain confident.
One thing I ask of you,
this is what I seek:
to know your will
every day of my life;
and seek from you, Higher Power,
the power to carry it out.
For you will give me shelter
in my times of trouble.
You will keep me safe in your arms;
you will set me on a high peak.
Now I can lift my head high
in the face of naysayers;
I will rejoice out loud
in your dwelling place.

I will sing and make music to you.

Hear me, God, when I shout out;

give heed to my cry and answer me.

My heart says, "Seek your God!"

God, I do seek you;

do not hide from me.

In your anger do not reject me;

for you are the one who helps me.

Do not despise me or ignore me,

for you are the one who saves me.

Even if my parents abandon me,

my Higher Power will not leave me.

Teach me the Steps, my God,

and keep me on a straight path,

safe from my obsessions.

Don't let me succumb to addictions,

which only seek to deceive me;

their path leads to my ruin.

I believe that I shall see your goodness

in people who are alive and well.

So I wait for you, my God.

My heart finds strength and courage

as I wait for my Higher Power.

PSALM 28

I call upon my Higher Power;

my rock, do not reject my plea.

If you refuse to listen to me,

I'll be like those swallowed by the earth.

Hear my voice raised in prayer,

when I come to you for help,

as I raise my hands in pleading

toward your dwelling place on high.

Preserve me from entrapment by my addiction,

from the temptations that can end my life,

who say one thing and do another,

who tell me lies and insist they are true.

May their falsehoods cause their failure,

trapping them in their deceits.

May their lies cause their collapse,

and give them their just due.

Because they pay no heed to you

or the great works of your hands,

your mighty works won't be enough to save them.

Blessed be my Higher Power,

who has heard the sound of my prayer.

You are my strength and my anchor,

my heart puts its trust in you;

thus I am helped, and I am glad,

and I give thanks to my Power on high.

God, you're the strength of us addicts,

you are the one who rescues us.

Come, save your people;

bless us all;

be a shepherd

who brings your lambs home.

PSALM 29

Children of a Higher Power,
give glory and praise to our God.
For in the midst of my stormy life
your voice intrudes like thunder.
Your voice is powerful;
your words are life.
Your words lift the burden
that lies heavy upon me.
They lift my spirit
so that I skip like a child.
You send forth light
that drives out my darkness.
My world is topsy-turvy,
and you set it right again.
Your words grab our attention;
when we follow the Steps,
we discover your grandeur.
You reign above the chaos,
through a lifetime of turmoil.
You give strength to us;
you grant us serenity.

PSALM 30

I praise you, God,
for you have raised me up,
and did not allow my disease
to overcome me.

Higher Power,

I called for your help,

and you have healed me.

I was at the bottom

when you pulled me up;

at the lowest point of my life

when you restored me.

Sing praise to our God,

all you who are in recovery,

and give thanks for God's power.

For God's anger only lasts a moment,

while favor toward us lasts a lifetime.

We may be sad for a while,

but joy is always nearby.

I once thought to myself,

"That could never happen to me."

I felt strong and secure in myself,

that I could never fall so low.

Then you disappeared

and I was shocked.

I cried out for you, God;

I pleaded for your aid.

I pointed out that

"You have nothing to gain

by letting me die!

My ashes could not praise you;

I'd be unable to speak well of you."

I asked you, "Show me your kindness;

come to me and help me."
You have changed my mourning to dancing;
the darkest clothing of my grief
is replaced with a wardrobe of joy.
Now I can praise you and not stay silent,
I will praise my Higher Power forever.

PSALM 31

I seek a safe shelter with you, God;
save me from my craving;
deliver me by your mighty power.
Listen to me, please,
and rescue me quickly.
Be a solid foundation for me,
a strong fortress that protects me.
You definitely are my rock and fortress.
Lead me so that people know your greatness;
pull me away from things that will ensnare me,
because you are the one who can rescue me.
I place myself in your hands,
knowing that you have saved me.
You hurt when people choose idols,
but I have chosen you.
I rejoice in your merciful healing
because you saved me in my affliction.
You noted the compulsions I suffered,
and did not allow my pain to continue;
you set me on a path to recovery.

I cry out to you in my agony,

my eyes are red from my weeping,

my mind and body are exhausted.

My life is awash in sorrow

after years of anguish;

My strength is gone due to misery;

my energy is spent.

There are many who pick on me,

and more who are horrified by my actions;

my friends dread to come near me,

and passersby turn their eyes.

I'm forgotten, as if I had died,

as if I'm something thrown in the trash.

People talk behind my back;

I'm paranoid and afraid.

They gossip and speak ill of me;

they hope I won't survive.

But still I trust in you, God;

you're my Higher Power.

My life is in your hands;

deliver me from the grasp of evil.

Turn your face toward me,

and gaze at me with love.

Don't let me give in to my craving;

that's what I ask of you.

Let the wicked fall by their evil;

let them drop into the realm of death.

Let the lies against me be silenced—

those who speak disrespectfully,

who have pride and contempt for me.

How generous is your goodness,

which you share lavishly with us.

You have done great things for us,

and others can see it is so.

Our shelter is in you,

who protect us from temptations;

you guard us from harmful desires.

Praise be to our Higher Power,

who has wondrously proved such love

when I was surrounded and harassed.

In my panic I thought you were gone;

but you heard my cry of distress.

Turn to God, all you addicts,

who has the power to save you;

and let the self-reliant fall.

Take courage and find your strength;

let your heart find your God.

PSALM 32

Blest are the ones whose

defects are pardoned.

Blest are those whose actions are forgiven,

who do not hide their past.

If I stay silent, I stay sick;

my history gnaws at my guts.

The load is heavy on my heart;

my strength is sapped by my silence.

I acknowledge my faults to you,

and I do not hide my defects.

I admit my wrongs to you,

and I receive your gift of mercy.

Let all who have shortcomings pray;

you will save us in our distress.

You are a safe shelter for us;

you protect us in times of trouble.

We shout out to you with gladness.

You will remove our character defects;

you will release us from our shortcomings.

You don't force yourself upon us,

or beat us down with threats and blows,

for then we'd just turn away.

We are tormented with this disease

but our recovery shows that you care.

All who are sober, rejoice,

and in your healing, shout for joy.

PSALM 33 *"you righteous"(ʋ/)*

1 We, the sober, rejoice in you;

Praise is fitting by those in recovery.

2 We praise you with stringed instruments;

we play melodies with guitar and harp.

3 We sing a new song to you *(him)*

and make our music skillfully.

4 For your *(YHWH's)* word is honest and true,

and your works are faithfully done.

5 (He)
You love integrity and justice;

you steadfastly love all creation.

6 The power of your (the Lord) word made the heavens,

which you filled with the moon and the stars.

7 You created the waters of the oceans;

you gathered the lakes and the streams.

8 Let the universe praise you, God;

let all who live stand in awe.

9 When you command, it happens;

when you speak, it comes to pass.

10 The good ideas of the nations

eventually come to nothing.

If we want to make you laugh,   " he frustrates the plans
we make plans.   of the people "

11 Your wisdom lasts forever;

the thoughts of your heart endure.

12 Blest are the people who trust in you,

for you make those people your legacy.

13 You look down from heaven

and see what has been made;

14 You see humanity from on high.

15 You know the human heart

and see our mortal deeds.

16 No one is saved by their weapons;

no human strength can save us.

17 A "fix" cannot fix our problems;   " a horse ... "
our power can't satisfy our needs.

18 You're attentive to us who trust your might,
who submit to a Higher Power

19 who can deliver us from our addiction, — *"soul from death"*
and keep us alive and sober. — *"alive in famine"*

20 And so we long for you, God,
for you are healing and safety. — *"our help and shield"*

21 Our hearts are grateful to you,
because we trust our Higher Power. — *"in his holy name"*

22 May your love fall upon us
who find our hope in you.

PSALM 34

I will always praise my Higher Power,
my mouth will offer you words of praise.
I boast about what you have done;
let those who hear be glad with me.
I looked for you, who answered me
and delivered me from my fears.
I turn to you, and let my face glow,
never clouded over by shame.
This wreck cried out; I was heard
and was saved from all my troubles.
My Higher Power sets up camp
in the lives of those who call.
We watch and see that you are good;
when you enter our lives we are safe.
Hold this Higher Power in awe,
for those who do so lack nothing.

When young we feel empty and hungry,
but those who find you are satisfied.
Children, gather round and listen;
hear about the wonder of God.
For who doesn't want to live,
to enjoy a long and happy life?
Then do not practice deceit
nor spread malicious lies.
Set aside evil, and do good;
desire peace, and make it real.
You look on those who seek your will,
and respond readily to their prayers.
You turn away from those who do evil,
so that no one will remember their deeds.
When the innocent call out, you hear them,
and deliver them from their troubles.
You stay close to the brokenhearted,
and those who are crushed you restore.
The innocent are often afflicted;
you deliver them from their distress.
You keep their bodies safe,
so no harm comes to them.
Evil leads to death for the wicked,
and condemns those who harm the innocent.
Our Higher Power saves those who submit;
those who follow your will are never lost.

PSALM 35

Challenge those, God, who challenge me;
fight those who fight against me.
Grab your weapons and defend me;
take up arms against those who can harm me.
Speak to my heart and say, "I will save you."
Take away the desires that will harm me;
remove the cravings that will destroy my life.
Let them be like fluff in the wind
as you drive them out of my life.
There was no reason to choose me;
I did nothing to deserve this disease.
Let it crumble before your Power;
may it self-destruct and vanish.
Then I shall rejoice in you,
and give praise for my salvation.
My whole being will shout,
"There's no one else like you!"
You rescue the weak,
for we cannot do it alone;
we are powerless to save ourselves.
Harmful desires attack me;
they do hurtful things to me.
My good deeds are repaid with evil,
and my spirit is weighed down with sorrow.
When others fell sick, I helped them;
I grieved for them and prayed.

I bowed my head to my chest,
mourned them like my own siblings.
I lamented as if they were my family,
bowed down with heartache and sorrow.
But when I stumbled, they laughed;
like young hoodlums, they mugged me.
They stood close by and mocked me,
and taunted me with false promises.
How long, God, will you stand by and watch?
Rescue me from these assaults,
save me from this violence.
Then I'll gather with others and thank you;
I'll praise you at meetings day and night.
Don't let my cravings undo me,
nor my obsessions deceive me.
They cannot provide true peace,
but only results that upset me.
They claim to speak the truth,
to know more than I know myself.
God, you've seen this again and again.
Don't stay quiet! Come close!
Step up to the bar! Plead my case;
seek justice for me, my God!
Support me through the Steps,
and do not let the addiction win!
May those who rejoice at my downfall
be put to shame themselves.
Let those who stand over me gloating

be humbled and disgraced in public.

While those who stand with me are happy,

and praise God who keeps me abstinent.

Then my mouth will speak of your goodness,

and sing your praises all the day long.

PSALM 36

My addiction speaks to me

in the core of my heart.

There is no fear of God there.

I so flatter myself in my mind

that I don't even recognize my illness.

I lie to myself and deceive myself.

Wisdom is gone; insanity has taken its place.

I think about my next X

even when I'm in bed.

I'm caught in the grip of my addiction.

I cling to it as if it were my lifeboat.

But you, God, are greater than my illness.

Your power is stronger than my addiction.

True sobriety is like a high mountain

and abstinence like the ocean's depth.

You give protection to all who need it;

how precious is your healing power.

God, in our addictions

we find shelter in you.

We can feast on your rich food

and drink from your stream of clean water.
For you are the real power of healing
and in your strength we can find sobriety.
Reach out to us and help us know you,
and do what is right for us all.
Do not allow our addictions to crush us,
nor society to cast us aside.
For we see what can happen to the addicted;
they can fall so far that they can't stand up again.

PSALM 37

1   I don't envy the addicted,
or feel jealous of their illness;

2   for they will wither like the grass
and dry up like uprooted weeds.

3   I trust in you, and do my Steps
so I'll live and enjoy sobriety.

4   I find pleasure in my Higher Power
who can give me my heart's desires.

5   I turn my life over to you;
give to you my self-powered will.

6   You light up the path to recovery,
and the way to sobriety is made clear.

7   I am still, and know you;
I wait patiently for your healing.
I don't worry about others
and what they're doing;
how they seem better than me.

8 I hand over my anger, not keep it;
   resentment only leads to more problems.

9 Those using will finally be cut off;
   but those who get sober will live. *"wait for the (LORD) shall inherit the Land"*

10 Some time will pass, and they'll die;
    though you tried to save them, they passed.

11 On the other hand, the humble have thrived;
    and found their lives better than ever.

12 Those using want to taint others;
    they taunt with pledges of relief.

13 But you laugh at their empty promises,
    knowing none of it will come to pass.

14 Cravings mount an attack
    to bring down the weak and the lost,
    to slaughter the fragile and helpless.

15 Their desires will be their own downfall;
    they will lose their own lives by their hands.

16 Better a day of abstinence
    than weeks of using X.

17 For those who use will fall;
    while you hold up the clean.

18 You count our days of sobriety,
    a legacy that lasts forever.

19 We no longer drop our heads in shame;
    in the face of temptation, we abstain.

20 The unrecovered addicts perish.
    Their dependence is falsely placed;
    they vanish like windblown smoke.

21 An addict borrows, but doesn't repay,
   while the sober are generous and kind.
22 Those who recover give service;
   but those who don't are self-centered.
23 Our Steps are made firm by you, God;
   you delight as we find our way.
24 Though we stumble, we will not fall,
   for you hold us up with your hand.
   I who was young am now old,
   I still see the recovering thrive.
   We give freely to others in need,
   and our children learn to do likewise.
   I trust God, and do the Steps
   so that I can stay alive.
   Yes, our God loves us forever,
   and will never disown the addicted.
   The recovering will admit they are wrong,
   and users will continue to lie.
   The sober will make their amends,
   while users will beg, borrow, and steal.
   The sober will carry your message
   as they maintain their contact with you.
   The sober will practice the principles;
   they stay firm in the path of Twelve Steps.
   The illness is alert for the weak,
   and seeks to destroy our lives.
   But you don't leave us to the disease,
   nor condemn us when we fall.

I wait for God, and follow the Steps,
and you will raise me up;
I will receive God's healing help.
I have felt addictive obsessions
take over like a field of weeds.
But then they disappear,
for God has entered the scene.
We become people who do not blame;
we're responsible for our own misdeeds.
We admit we have some shortcomings
and we ask you to remove our defects.
Salvation comes to the sober;
you rescue us when we're in trouble.
You save us when we're powerless;
you help us to manage our days
when we turn over our will and our lives.

PSALM 38

God, do not show spite toward me,
or direct harsh discipline at me.
I have already felt your heat
and your heavy hand upon me.
I suffer with this dreadful disease
because I have not turned to you;
I suffer unnecessarily
because of my own decisions.
The results of my choices
weigh on me heavily.

My wounds get worse and fester
because of my foolishness.
I am laid low to the ground;
I drag myself around all day.
My guts are burning
and my flesh decays.
I am worn out and bruised;
I groan from a broken heart.
God, you know my longing;
you are not deaf to my groaning.
My heart is pounding
and my strength failing;
the light of my eyes has gone dim.
My friends and family move away from me;
my neighbors shun my affliction.
My addiction has trapped me;
it will take my life
if I don't change.
But like the deaf, I do not hear;
like the mute, I don't ask for help.
I cover my ears to avoid advice
and make no response to goodwill.
I continue to wait for you, God;
I know you will answer me soon.
My prayer is that my addiction passes
and doesn't grab me again if I slip.
For I know I may fall more than once;
my pain is always at my side.

I admit my wrongdoing
and acknowledge my weakness.
My cravings are relentless foes
and my temptations taunt me.
They urge me to make bad choices
and make my illness worse.
God, do not abandon me!
Don't keep your distance from me.
Make haste to help me, Higher Power;
You're the only one who can heal me.

PSALM 39

I stayed quiet for a long time;
I kept my thoughts to myself.
I thought I could preserve the peace
if only I kept my mouth shut.
I stayed silent and still;
I kept my peace, but it didn't work.
My sorrow increased,
and my heart wore out.
While I kept quiet, a fire burned inside,
until I could hold it in no longer:
I know some day I'll die;
I don't know how or when;
let me remember that life is short.
Life is only a matter of years,
which is a flash of time for you;
for you our lives are just a moment.

s like a shadow;

l for no good reason;

ho will reap the reward?

All I can do is wait for you;

You are the one I hope for.

Rescue me from my weakness

and save me from my addiction.

I am quiet and say nothing,

but I really think this is your fault!

Stop punishing me;

I can't take any more.

Perhaps it's fair that you punish us,

for we use—destroying your beloved,

wasting away because of this disease.

Hear my prayer, Higher Power;

listen to my pleas, please;

do not withhold your peace.

For my life is passing away;

I'm a stranger, unknown to you.

Back off for a time

so that I can regain some strength

before I leave this earth.

PSALM 40

I waited patiently for you, God,

who turned toward me and heard my plea.

You pulled me

out of the pit of horrors,

out of the swamp of sewage.
You set me safely on firm ground,
and showed me the Steps to take.
My Higher Power gave me a song,
new music to praise you, my God.
Those who put their trust in you—
who are not arrogant,
who don't chase idols—
are healed.
Your good deeds and thoughts of us
have multiplied your blessings.
If I were to count them off,
the number would be too great.
You don't want my sacrifices
and meaningless words or oaths;
You don't extract empty promises,
asking only for open hearts.
I sought you out in prayer;
I made conscious contact with you.
Now I delight to do your will;
with your grace I carry it out.
I tell about my recovery;
I speak of you in meetings.
I don't hold back my thoughts—
you know that this is true.
I don't hide what has happened;
I share my hope with others.
I don't conceal my history

or the story of your healing.
Don't hold back your mercy;
let your forgiveness save my soul.
For addictions besiege me
and my wrongs overwhelm me.
My shortcomings are numerous;
my defects slash my heart.
Find it in your heart to help me;
God, make haste to save me.
Heave to the belly of the earth
these obsessions that drag down my life.
Let those people suffer
who delight in my pain.
Let those who revel in my misery
see the harm their words have caused me.
May all who seek you be glad
for their joy in finding your strength;
may all who have found your healing
say, "My Higher Power is great!"
In all humility I pray this,
for my recovery is all your doing.
You are my help and my savior;
come quickly, and stay close.

PSALM 41

It is good to pray for those who are weak;
You deliver them when they're in trouble.
You preserve them and keep them alive;

they are grateful for your compassionate care.
Some look forward to the day that they'll die;
but you sustain them on their sickbed;
you bring healing to their illness.
I prayed, "God, give me your grace, and heal me;
this disease has harmed me and my family."
Yes, those with hard hearts wait for my death,
gleeful that I may die and be forgotten.
Their visits are short; their words are empty;
when they depart, they spread gossip about me.
They enjoy imagining the worst for me.
They think I have a deadly illness,
and that I will never recover.
Even my closest friend has walked away.
But you show grace and raise me up.
This shows me that I delight you,
and my friends are wrong about you.
You pull me up because of my integrity;
you give me a favored place at your side.
God, you are great for all time. So it is.

PSALM 42

Like an animal on the prowl,
I am looking for something.
I'm looking for a power
greater than myself.
When will I find such a power?
I'm so upset I cannot eat,

wondering if there's a Higher Power?
I remember how it used to be—
how I used to stand up front,
shouting about my success,
hanging out with successful people.
Then why am I so whipped?
Why can't I catch a break?
"Hope in God!"
Someday I'll find my God,
whose power can save me.
My heart is broken because
I remember how it used to be—
how I traveled and saw the views,
mountains and oceans and stars.
Each day my God still loves me,
at night God sings a lullaby,
a song of a life of serenity.
I ask my God, "Why?
Why have you forgotten me?
Why must I live with this grief
because of the disease in my life?"
It's a permanent wound to my heart,
a heartache that will not stop:
I keep wondering to myself,
"Is there a Higher Power?"
Then why am I so whipped?
Why can't I catch a break?
"Hope in God!"

Someday I'll find my God,
whose power can save me.

PSALM 43

Hear my case; proclaim my innocence
before a jury of my peers:
I did nothing to deserve this disease.
I want a decision: "Not guilty!"
Why do you push me away?
Why must I live with this grief
because of the disease in my life?
Issue a truthful decision;
free me from what confines me.
Then I'll proclaim it aloud;
all will know my joy,
all will hear my praise:
"God is my Higher Power!"
But for now I ask you, God,
"Why have you forgotten me?
Why must I live with this grief
because of the disease in my life?"

PSALM 44

We've been told at Twelve-Step meetings;
we have heard it with our own ears:
what marvelous things you have done.
You drove out an awful disease;
you freed those caught in addiction.

We did not do this ourselves;
our own efforts did not save us.
It was your strength
and your wisdom,
for we delighted you.
You are my God, my Higher Power;
you make the victories occur.
We push away the compulsions through you;
we maintain our sobriety through you.
We do not trust our stinkin' thinkin',
nor place our trust in personal strength.
You are the one who saves us
and drives out our crazy obsessions.
We boast at meetings about what you've done,
and give thanks every day of our lives.
When we strike out on our own
you let us fall and harm ourselves.
The addiction rears its head again
and messes up our lives once more.
We are like sheep headed for slaughter,
headed straight toward the pit of death.
You let us go, and we pay the price;
we feel the scorn of family and friends.
We're a laughingstock among neighbors;
we feel our disgrace and our shame.
The words of judgment haunt us;
the names they call us touch our core.
Despite all that has happened,

we have not forgotten you,
or the promises you have made.
Our hearts are still made for you,
and the Steps still lead to you.
But we're broken and in danger;
we're lost in a hostile darkness.
If we had really forgotten you,
wouldn't you already know it?
Yet we have turned to a false god.
You know our deepest desires.
You know we're slowly dying
like sheep being led to slaughter.
Wake up, God! Rouse yourself,
and do not let me slip away.
Don't turn your face away from me;
don't hide from my affliction.
I am falling to the ground,
sinking in the quicksand.
Get up, God! Come, help me!
Save me because you love me.

PSALM 45

My heart overflows with emotion:
I address myself to you, my God.
My tongue is sharp and ready.
You are the Highest of all Powers,
and grace comes easily from your lips.
Wherever you are, there is blessing.

Day by day you bring victories
for the sake of goodness and truth.
Your mighty hand does great deeds;
you achieve what you set out to do.
Your reign will last forever:
you always strive for equity;
you love goodness and hate evil.
You are the Anointed One:
you shine with the oil of gladness.
You have the odor of holiness.
You are pleased by the beauty of music.
Your servants gather round you;
the lowly and the great surround you.
Listen up, people!
We must learn to forget ourselves!
God already sees our beauty.
Because God is the Highest Power,
we must learn to trust our God,
to seek the reign of God,
to attain the riches of God.
We must learn to clothe ourselves
with the goodness of sobriety
and the beauty of serenity.
We must learn to follow the Steps
and believe God's eternal promises;
we must follow the will of God.
Then we'll wake up spiritually.
We'll practice the principles daily,
and carry this message to others.

PSALM 46

God,

you are my refuge,

my source of strength.

So I'm not afraid,

even if my world is shaken,

and the floodwaters come,

and the skies thunderclap.

God, you're like a river,

flowing through our minds,

refreshing our lives each day.

There's uproar all around us;

the world is falling apart.

Still you shelter us in safety.

Look at what you have done!

Turmoil has come to an end;

what once wreaked havoc now brings peace.

Be still!

We come close to meet you.

We learn to love and thank you.

The God of the universe is here!

You shelter us in safety.

PSALM 47

Applause!

We give you a round of applause

for you are the Most High Power!

You are the most awesome Power of all!

You bring addictions to subjection;
you subdue our strongest cravings.
You create a bright future for us,
for we are your pride and joy.
You stand tall among us.
A trumpet blast announces you're here.
We jump to our feet in excitement;
our Higher Power is here!
You are the Most High Power,
and you make your home among us.
We addicts gather with you
and count on your mighty strength.
You are the Great Protector
and we find our safety in you.

PSALM 48

God, you're great and should be praised.
Out in the country and in the cities,
on the mountains and in the valleys,
north and south, east and west,
in all corners of the world—you save us.
Addicts came together and were astounded;
they spoke of what you'd done for so many.
Others were panicked and ran away;
they wouldn't believe what you could do.
They trembled in fear
and shook in their shoes.
We've seen and heard it repeatedly;

it's true in our own experience.
We ponder your committed love,
God, in the midst of addiction.
Your power reaches out
to the people furthest away.
You offer us recovery.
We rejoice and are glad
because your judgment is *mercy*
and we are not forgotten.
I think about my life:
as I look at it from all directions,
I consider how strong I was,
how I thought I was in control!
Then I tell my story again,
how I found my Higher Power;
I speak about what God has done
and will continue to do forever.

PSALM 49

Hear this, all those in trouble;
listen up, all addicts in the world,
high and low, rich and poor—
my mouth shall offer prayer.
I will meditate and seek God's wisdom.
I will seek conscious contact with you,
I will pray for knowledge of your will.
Why should I fear on troubled days,
when the cravings of my addiction attack me,

when they promise me relief
and abundance of good times?
They cannot save my life;
they cannot provide what only you can give.
(I would pay a high price and gain nothing,
believing my life had been spared.)
We who use (and who don't) will die;
whether using or recovering, we'll perish,
and all possessions are left behind.
Whatever our wealth, there's a grave;
a place in the earth awaits us,
no matter how much we own.
Titles and honors won't matter;
like all flesh we will succumb.
This is the fate of the foolish,
who refuse to think of their future.
Like sheep they are destined for death,
and addiction will be their shepherd;
they are headed straight for a grave,
their bodies shall waste away,
and a tomb will be their abode.
But you will save me from death,
for you will gather me home.
I won't be afraid when some become rich,
when the list of their assets increases.
When they die they'll carry nothing,
their wealth will not follow them.
In their lifetime they thought they were fine—

that's what we think when all's well—
they'll join the other fools
who failed to see the light.
Titles and honors won't matter;
like all flesh we will succumb.

PSALM 50

Our Higher Power speaks,
your voice, to the ends of the earth.
You shine forth in the beauty
of those who are recovering.
You come and do not keep silent;
you move in a fury
and a swirl of activity.
Our Higher Power gets involved
to save those who are struggling:
"Gather to me those who are hurting,
those who've made promises to quit."
Everyone knows this bodes well,
for our Higher Power is strong.
"Listen to me, you addicts;
pay attention to my message,
for I am God, who can save you.
I don't rebuke you for your promises,
nor your efforts to save yourselves.
I don't need your sacrifices,
nor your good deeds, nor your gifts.
For everything that exists is mine.

If I were hungry, I wouldn't tell you:

you have nothing to give that's not mine;

I don't need your food and your wine.

Bring to me a gift of gratitude,

and keep your promise to abstain.

Ask for my help when you're troubled;

I'll deliver you, and you'll thank me."

But to those still using, God says,

"What right do you have to quote me,

to cite the promises I've made?

For you hate any form of self-discipline,

and you ignore what I have taught you.

You persist in your use of X,

and you hang out with those who are using.

Your mouth keeps spouting off,

and your tongue continues to lie.

You harm yourselves and your families;

you deceive them and cause them more pain.

I've stayed quiet through all your nonsense,

perhaps you thought I had disappeared.

But I have been with you, always,

and now I tell you the truth.

So listen, you who've forgotten me,

or you'll crash and burn to ash,

and no one will be there to save you.

You who listen and abstain,

you will be filled with thanksgiving,

for I am the God who saves you."

PSALM 51

Have mercy on me, God;

in your loving-kindness show mercy.

Blot out my addiction

and cleanse me from my sin.

For I truly know this disease;

it's in my face every day.

I have failed you over and over

and done what I know was wrong.

You'd be justified to pass judgment

and condemn me once and for all.

I have been sick for so long

I can hardly recall being well.

You look for integrity of heart;

then in my heart teach me wisdom.

Heal me of this illness;

make my life clean again.

Let my ears hear laughter,

and my body feel refreshed.

Don't look at my wrongdoings;

blot out my shortcomings.

Create a clean heart in me, God,

put a fresh spirit within me.

Don't ever push me away,

or let me think you hate me.

Restore the joy of feeling young,

and help me to follow your will.

Then I'll carry this message to others,

so that they can recover too.
Save me from harm and violence;
then I'll speak of your deliverance.
Put the right words in my mouth
so I can dutifully praise you.
I don't have to make weird promises;
there's nothing in that which pleases you.
What's pleasing is my abstinence,
and a humility that relies on you.
It's your pleasure to heal us,
to help us rebuild our lives.
You'll delight in our sobriety
and the offering of our will.

PSALM 52

You think you're so high and mighty,
just because you can knock others down.
You slay people with your tongue,
and lie more than tell the truth.
You enjoy hurting others,
and delight in deceit.
But God will bring you down;
God will pluck you from your place of safety;
your life will no longer be your own.
Those who seek the truth will see this;
we'll be glad to see what's come of you.
As an addict you only trust yourself,
and sooner or later you'll bottom out.
On the other hand, I'm thriving;

I found a Higher Power
whose strength is greater than mine.
I will always be grateful
for what God has done for me.
I will declare this at my meetings
and carry this message to others.

PSALM 53

We fools tell ourselves, "There is no God.
There is no one who can save me."
And so we remain in our addiction,
and nothing good develops.
But God is on high alert,
watchful for those who want sanity,
ready to admit they are powerless.
Sometimes we cannot see
how far we have fallen;
our lives are unmanageable.
We do not yet believe
there's a Power who can save us.
We do not believe you, God.
And so we live in fear,
and our fears increase.
Our bodies wear out from stress
and the damage caused by X.
Despite our blindness, come!
Deliver us from our fear;
help us to know you as you are.

PSALM 54

Rescue me, Higher Power;
use your strength to save me.
Listen to my plea for help,
and hear my desperation.
My addiction seems stronger than ever;
relentlessly it assaults me.
I cannot find you, God, to save me.
I trust that you are here,
even if I cannot feel you.
I believe you can relieve my distress
and heal my compulsions.
I will turn over my will to you,
and submit my life to your care.
For you'll deliver me from my problems;
I'll rejoice in my deep healing.

PSALM 55

Listen to me, God,
and don't cover your ears.
Pay attention to my request
because I'm really bothered.
I'm upset by my head-noise,
the insanity filling my mind.
My thoughts get me in trouble,
and my behavior makes things worse.
My heart is in deep anguish,
and the threat of death stands near.

Fear and anger fill my head;

resentments overwhelm me.

I think, "If I had wings,

I'd fly from this mess.

I'd fly as high and as far as possible,

so that I'd finally find some peace.

I'd look for a quiet place that is safe

where I'm no longer plagued by these thoughts."

You see the state of affairs;

you know the confusion in my head.

Night and day the chaos persists;

and I keep making bad choices.

The disease has taken over

and I may not survive it.

I had no plan to be addicted;

who'd ever want such a thing?

My friends were fellow users,

and we thought we had no problem.

Once I thought X was my friend;

I could count on X

to lessen my pain,

help me forget,

make me feel better.

But now X has turned against me,

no longer a useful companion.

I beg you to kill this addiction;

stomp it into the dust,

for it's killing my heart and soul.

I call on my Higher Power,
and believe that you will save me.
Morning, noon, and night I pray;
I beg you to hear my voice.
You will rescue me from this battle,
from the forces stacked against me.
God on high, you'll heal me,
and destroy those lethal powers;
I cannot do it myself;
only you can save me.
Some friends said they'd stand by me;
they broke their promise to me.
Their words were sweet to my hearing,
but their actions hurt me deeply.
They said what I wanted to hear,
and then they walked away.
Now I turn to you, God;
I count on your word.
You will keep your promise;
you will not forget.
You will heal my defects
and correct my shortcomings;
my wrongs will be forgiven
and set aside forever.
I will trust your will each day,
and do my best to carry it out.

PSALM 56

Give me your grace today
to push back the cravings
that surely will come my way.
Temptations assault me;
they infect my mind.
Higher Power, protect me
as I place my trust in you.
God, I trust your will; I am not afraid;
my addictions will not be victorious.
Every day they attract me;
my thoughts keep returning to X.
They lurk in the shadows,
arouse my fears and
stir up my anger.
I want healing for my feelings
so they do not defeat my life.
You can track my turmoil;
you can count my tears;
your accounting is true.
When I call on you,
my cravings go away—
you do this for me.
God, I trust your will; I thank you.
I trust the Steps; I am not afraid.
My addictions will not be victorious.
I promise to follow the Steps,

and always be grateful to you.
You have saved me from death,
from an endless life of hell,
so that I can live
one day at a time.

PSALM 57

Have mercy on me, God;
show your mercy, as I
seek my healing from you.
Give me protective cover
from the storms that assault me.
I call on my Higher Power
whose desire is my serenity.
From on high you will reach out
to rescue me from my torment.
Your steadfast love, my God,
will always be faithful.
I'm caught amid temptations
that try to devour me;
Razor sharp are the cravings
that attack my body and mind.
My Higher Power is mighty;
your strength can heal the whole earth.
This disease tries to trip up my Steps;
my body bows down with exhaustion.
The road is filled with potholes
that make me stumble and fall.

My heart is steadfast, God,

as I take one day at a time.

I will make music and sing,

as my whole being awakes.

Wake up, guitar and harp;

wake up, sleepy world!

I'll express my gratitude to you,

and speak of your love to the nations.

Your steadfast love is powerful,

and your fidelity lasts forever.

My Higher Power is mighty;

your strength can heal the whole earth.

PSALM 58

Is there any addiction in the universe

that has my well-being at heart,

whose only ambition is justice?

I don't think so!

Most often their focus is themselves,

and their only goal is their relief.

Their selfishness begins at birth

with little interruption thereafter.

Their self-interest is like a poison

that taints every word from their mouths.

Their ears cannot hear honesty,

and they know nothing of kindness.

Break the teeth in their mouths;

destroy their tongues of deceit.

Make addictions like dew that vanishes,
like grass that is trampled on and dies.
Make them like creatures living in slime,
like misshapen monsters destined to die.
Before they delight in the daylight
sweep them away into darkness.
Those who do justice rejoice;
they see you subdue evil.
They note that "justice is rewarded,
and you honor those who are honest."

PSALM 59

God, save me from my addiction,
from powers that will destroy me.
Free me from deadly cravings,
from urges that will end my life.
They lie in wait to trip me,
they stir up trouble that harms me.
This disease is not my fault;
I assert my innocence.
Get up, God, and come to my aid.
Almighty One and Higher Power,
Rouse yourself, and wipe out my illness;
spare nothing that gets in the way.
Each night the desires return,
like dogs that sniff out weakness.
They know my soft spots and attack;

they corrupt my thoughts with insanity.
You laugh at my silly ideas;
you know they're really foolish.
I wait for you, my God,
because you are my strength.
Your steady love will lead me;
your strength will guide my healing.
My healing will never be finished;
my recovery remains in your hands.
As long as my pride remains,
there is no room for humility.
As long as I deceive myself,
there is no space for honesty.
As long as I rely on you,
there is hope to regain my sanity.
Each night the urges return,
sniffing out my weakness.
They're on alert for soft spots,
and growl when they don't succeed.
In the morning I celebrate abstinence;
one more day I rejoice in your power.
You give me saving strength,
and when I need it, grace.
Higher Power, I thank you;
my God, you are my strength,
the source of constant love.

PSALM 60

God, I feel like you've rejected me;
you're angry and my defenses are down.
I'm standing at the edge of a cliff;
the land is giving way under me.
You've caused me to suffer greatly;
you've given me more than I can handle.
You hang out a flag to attract me,
to rally my heart that's distressed.
You grant victory to those who submit,
who know your will and then follow it.
My joyful God has promised healing:
"I'll give you hope and perseverance,
honesty, faith, and forgiveness.
Abstinence is yours;
serenity is my gift.
I'll drive out fear, wash away anger,
and triumph over resentments."
Who will lead me to a safe place?
Who can manage my feelings?
Have you rejected me, God?
Have you abandoned me to my disease?
Give me your healing for this illness,
because all human aid is worthless.
With you I shall succeed,
for only you have the power.

PSALM 61

Hear my cry, my God;
listen to my prayer.
I call to you from a distance;
my heart is weary.
Take me to a high spot,
where you can rescue me.
You are my Higher Power,
someone greater than me.
Let me always dwell in your love,
and find my sobriety with you.
You know my intentions are strong;
you give hope to all who trust you.
May those in recovery have long lives;
may abstinence endure for a lifetime.
May they always put trust in you, God,
who are constant and faithful in love.
And so I'll be grateful to you,
and follow one day at a time.

PSALM 62

My whole being is waiting
in silent anticipation;
waiting for God, my rock,
my hope and my salvation.
I've been assaulted by my addiction,
tormented by my affliction,

assaulted by my obsession.

It drags me down
with false promises;
it offers relief
that never lasts.

My whole being is waiting
in silent anticipation;
waiting for God, my rock,
my hope and my salvation
I trust in you at all times;
I pour out my troubles to you,
the one who cares for me.

My birthplace doesn't matter;
my status is of no concern;
riches and poverty—so what?
nothing lasts; it's all dust.

Money is not power;
power is not strength.
I don't trust what cannot last.

This I've heard;
I know it's true:
Only you have power;
my only strength is you.
You are the one who restores
those who follow your will.

PSALM 63

God, you are the power I seek;

my whole being yearns for you.

My body longs for you

like an ever-thirsty desert.

I look for holy places

to see your boundless glory.

To have your love and your healing

is better than life itself;

how could I not praise you!

So I'll thank you as long as I live;

I'll clap my hands and shout your name.

I am filled with you,

content, as after a feast.

Even at night in my bed,

I can't stop thinking of you,

because you healed me,

and gave me joy again.

I have to stay close to you,

and I feel you hold me close.

There are some who want me to fail,

but they themselves will fall.

Their desires will be their downfall;

their lives will be lost to failures.

But we addicts will celebrate you;

we'll swear by your goodness and truth,

and the tongues of liars will be silenced.

PSALM 64

Listen to me, God, as I complain:
rescue my life from this dreadful disease.
Save me from its schemes—
it corrupts my simple mind;
it deceives me with lies,
and beats me with guilt and shame.
It has a life of its own,
and tries to trip me up.
I cannot see it; it hides,
then rears its ugly head.
It distorts the truth, and succeeds,
because the human mind is deep.
But you can get to the roots,
and mortally wound its plots.
You always speak the truth;
you drag its deceit into light.
All will see what you have done,
and reflect upon their healing.
Those who are saved will rejoice,
and keep conscious contact with you.

PSALM 65

Gratitude is your due, my God,
as I decide to follow the Steps.
My life cannot be managed
until I turn over my will to you.
I honestly search my history

and admit my wrongdoing.

I stand before you without fear,

and stay close to you in prayer.

When shortcomings overwhelm me,

you remove my defects of character.

You are the hope of all

who think their cause is lost.

You give me a foundation as firm as a mountain;

you silence the waves that roar in my ears.

In lands distant and close people hear of your deeds;

from east to west they shout for joy.

You rain on my drought and till my soil;

you prepare the earth to receive your seeds;

you enrich my soil, and plant the grain;

you bless it all and gather a harvest.

The wilderness overflows

and wildflowers bloom.

Flocks are plentiful

and pastures are full.

All this you do to bring me joy.

PSALM 66

Make some joyful noise for God!

Give thanks to God with joy!

I say, "Your deeds are great!

Because of your great power

I now enjoy recovery."

People in every land are grateful,

and make thanksgiving to you.
Come and hear what God is doing;
what awesome healing God has done.
The floods have dried up;
my journey is made safe.
And so we give you thanks
as you save us by your power.
You watch over us all,
and keep the humble safe.
Show God your gratitude, all people,
let the earth be filled with thanksgiving,
who keeps us among the living,
not allowing us to slip and fall.
We have been tested, for sure,
each day new temptations come—
nets of longing ensnare us;
burdens are laid on our backs;
people stomp on our ideas;
we're tempted by our cravings.
And through it all
you lead us to serenity.
I want to give you something
to repay you for your goodness.
All I can do is keep abstinence,
a promise I made when I "bottomed."
I offer to you my will,
and hand over to you my life.
Come and hear what God has done;

I'll say what God has done for me.

I cried out to God when all seemed lost,

and now I'm grateful, for I was saved.

If I hadn't admitted my wrongs,

there was nothing that you could do.

But you have heard my confession,

and listened to my prayer.

You forgive my wrongdoing,

and love me to the end.

PSALM 67

God, bless us with your grace;

look on us with kindness.

Let your will be known,

your desires for all your people.

Let all people thank you,

and be grateful for your love.

Let all nations be grateful

for you judge us with compassion.

Let all people thank you,

and be grateful for your love.

The addicted now thrive;

this is your work.

Keep healing us,

so every nation thanks you.

PSALM 68

Rise up, God!

Crush my compulsions.

Drive out my addictions.

May they vanish like smoke.

May they melt away like wax.

Let those in recovery exult,

and offer their thanks to you.

Let those who abstain rejoice.

Sing a song of praise to God,

who soars with the clouds.

Exult in our Higher Power,

whose might is greater than ours.

God of the pain-filled and lonely,

God of the sober and healthy—

you make a home for us all.

You lead us out of addiction

while others still cling to their X.

You are the one who guides us,

who leads us through our desert.

You are present in our earthquakes;

and stay with us in our storms.

You send rain to us when we're parched,

and sun when we're covered by darkness;

a dwelling place when we're lost.

You provide for our needs when we're drained.

Our Higher Power gives life;

we spread the message of healing:

You care! And restore us to sanity.

Healing comes when we follow the Program:

abstinence takes roots in our hearts;

sobriety helps us to thrive;

serenity gives us wings like a dove.

Others look at us with envy:

they see how we have grown;

they note our spiritual progress;

they see how you guide our lives.

You entered our lives with power

when we decided to make room for you.

You bring us with you

to the top of a mountain.

This is our gift to you:

we no longer push you away.

You sustain us each day with strength;

you are our daily healing.

You are the Power who preserves us,

our God who saves us from death.

You will shatter our addictions,

while we cover our heads with guilt.

You promise to bring us back,

to pull us from the depths.

You will wash us clean;

you will make us free.

People will line up to hear

our excitement when we declare

at meetings what you have done—

for the young and long-lived,

for followers and leaders,

for skeptics and believers.

Show your strength again

as you've already done so well.

Let newcomers receive the gift

of hearing that there is hope.

Destroy their dependencies

and conquer their compulsions.

Trample their temptations

and defeat their distorted desires.

Overpower their false idols

so they may turn to you.

All people, sing to God;

and all nations, give thanks.

Our Higher Power speaks

and guides with mighty words.

You reign over all

who follow your will.

Praise our God who is awesome,

who gives power and strength to all people.

PSALM 69

Save me, God,

for the floodwaters are up to my neck.

I sink into the swampy muck;

I cannot find a foothold.

The water is so deep;

the flood sweeps over my head.
I am weary from my crying
and my throat is dry.
My eyes grow heavy
as I wait for you, God.
I can't begin to count
the ways my life is messed up.
So many things drag me down;
I cannot manage my life.
Although I'm falsely accused,
you also know my faults;
my mistakes are not hidden from you.
Don't let me cause others shame,
God Most High;
Don't let those who seek sobriety
be harmed by my failures,
my saving God.
I have such a desire to surrender to you,
yet I hear the taunts of my temptations.
As I try to live with humility,
I am hit with accusations.
When I strive to live by the truth,
deceptions arise in my mind.
The people around me gossip,
and point out all my flaws.
Yet I pray to you, my God;
when you're ready, answer me.
When the time is right, heal me

because of your abundant love.
Rescue me from the swampy muck;
pull me out of the floodwaters.
Do not let the torrent sweep o'er me,
nor let me be swallowed by the pit.
Answer me, Higher Power,
for your loving-kindness is good;
turn toward me with tender mercy.
Do not hide your face from me,
because I'm in great distress;
answer me quickly.
Draw close to me; save me;
set me free from my addictions.
You know the insults I have suffered;
you know the shame I have felt;
my weaknesses are well known to you.
Slurs have broken my heart,
they weigh heavy on my soul.
I looked for kindness, but there was none;
I searched for comfort, and received nothing.
Instead of sympathy I heard a poisoned tongue;
instead of solace I heard only bitter words.
Let their bounty be their own trap,
and a snare for their friends.
Let their eyes go dark with cataracts,
and make their intestines rumble constantly.
Pour out your punishment upon them,
and let your anger annihilate them.

May their homes become places of bleakness,
so that no one wants to live there.
For they strike those already broken;
those who are wounded they attack again.
Let them feel guilt, and then some more;
do not let them off the hook.
Do not remember their good deeds;
wipe your memory of their virtue.
Turn to me, God, and protect me,
because I am in pain in distress.
My sobriety will be my praise;
my recovery will show my gratitude.
It will please you more than sacrifices,
and mean more than empty promises.
Let those still suffering see these things;
revive their hearts and let them find you.
For the Most High hears the desperate,
and does not abandon those in bondage.
Let the heavens and earth praise God,
as well as the seas and all their creatures.
For God will save the addicted
and help us rebuild our lives.
We come to our meetings with gratitude;
our families rejoice at our well-being;
those who surrender become fully alive.

PSALM 70

My God, be pleased to free me;
Higher Power, be quick to help me.
My addictions bring me confusion and shame;
let the attraction be horror to my eyes.
Let the desires that lure my mind
be turned into thoughts that disgust me.
Let all who seek you find you,
and come to believe in your power.
Let those who are restored praise you,
and turn their lives over to you.
Because I am lost and in trouble,
hurry to help me, God.
You are the one who can restore me;
Higher Power, don't delay!

PSALM 71

God, I want your protection;
don't disappoint me.
In your goodness deliver me;
turn toward me and hear me.
Be my place of shelter,
a fortress to protect me,
for you are my safety and strength.
Rescue me from my addictions,
from the grasp of my compulsions.
I've put my hope in you, my God,
since I was young.

I have leaned on you
since the day I was born,
when you drew me out
from my mother's womb.
My life is a red flag to others,
but you still keep me close.
My mouth is filled with praise,
with gratitude all day long.
When I get old, don't push me away;
don't forget me as my body wears out.
Cravings thrive in my weary flesh,
and desires pursue me without rest;
they act as if no one will save me.
God, do not keep your distance;
Higher Power, be quick to help me.
Let my addictions themselves be consumed,
for they lead to my shame and my harm.
I will keep hoping in you
and be thankful all the more.
I will speak of your healing power,
of the many ways you have saved me.
The number is too high to count
as I recount your mighty deeds.
You have taught me since I was young,
years later I continue to learn.
Do not even forget me
when I'm old and gray,
for I continue to proclaim your feats

to all generations who follow me:
your power and your goodness
reach to the highest heavens.
You have performed great deeds;
no one measures up to you.
I have seen many troubles in my life
and yet you let me live.
No matter how far I've fallen,
you pull me back to my feet.
I am truly honored by you
and comforted by your love.
I thank you, God, for your faithfulness,
with stringed instruments I praise you.
I play my guitar to make music;
thus I pray to my Higher Power.
My lips speak with joy as I thank you;
my whole being is grateful to you.
Each day I talk of your healing,
and the harmful things pass away.

PSALM 72

God, I ask for your healing
for myself and for my family.
Bring healing to all the addicted,
to all who are dependent.
May the lands be filled with healing,
and all nations enjoy sobriety.
May you ease the deep pain

of all who are suffering:
deliver them from their disease,
and crush their compulsions.
May they live as long as the sun,
survive until the moon fades away.
May you refresh the people worn down,
like water that nourishes grass.
May the world be filled with healing,
and serenity 'til the universe ends.
May sobriety extend its dominion
to every corner of the earth.
May everyone know your power,
that nothing is greater than you.
The addicted will know it is you
who alone can restore us to sanity.
All addicts will be ready and willing
to turn over our lives to your care.
We'll seek to know your will
and the power to carry it out.
For you help us in our great need,
when we suffer and call out to you.
You have mercy on the weak and the struggling,
and save the lives of those who are striving.
You redeem the stressed and dependent,
and set free the oppressed and abused.
The recovering addicts will live.
They'll enjoy prosperity again.
They'll awake to a new spiritual time,

and be blessed every day of their lives.
May their families be healed,
and their friendships be strengthened.
May new relationships bloom,
and strangers find welcome.
May they carry the message
and practice the Steps.
May their names be remembered
as those blessed by God.

PSALM 73

Yes, God is good to the honest,
to those who are pure in heart.
But I stumbled and fell ill,
and refused to follow the Steps.
I envy those who can use
and never be the worse for wear.
They feel no pain when they use,
and their bodies stay healthy and strong.
Their use doesn't get them in trouble;
it's not a plague as it is for me.
They can feel great pride
while looking down on me.
They can increase their wealth
and spend their money foolishly.
They speak and judge with malice
and threaten to cause harm to the weak.
They speak as if there's no God,

as if success is of their own doing.

Some people fall for their act,

and do not see their faults.

They think there is no God,

no Higher Power than themselves.

Such people know no better;

they're at ease and living high.

As much as I try to live humbly

and try to keep my hands clean,

it appears that I am punished,

and every day I'm afflicted.

If I think, "I'll choose my own path,"

I'd be untrue to the way you have shown.

I thought 'twas too hard,

when told the Twelve Steps;

then I prayed, and I learned

what my Higher Power can do.

You can put my addictions to death,

and bring an end to my dependence.

You can destroy them in a moment,

and sweep them away with your might.

When I awake, it'll seem like a dream,

and a new life will emerge in its place.

When I was sick and bitter,

when I felt stabbed in the back,

I was acting out of ignorance

and behaved like a buffoon.

But you are still with me;

you hold me by the hand.
You guide me with your wisdom
and honor me with your love.
Who else is there but you?
There is nothing else to want.
If my body gives out
and my heart starts to fail,
you'll still be my strength
and I'll love you forever.
Others may never find you,
and they'll die still unfulfilled.
But it's good for me to stay close,
and each day to do your will.

PSALM 74

God, why have you abandoned us?
Why do you stay angry at your people?
Remember how you saved us long ago,
how you redeemed us from our addictions?
Do you remember how close you were,
a part of our everyday lives?
But now that we've failed to abstain,
you seem distant and angry again.
We're attacked by reckless cravings,
consumed by distorted desires;
we're wracked with longings,
and infected with needs.
We burn with obsessions;

we're being destroyed.
We're slammed to the ground
and consumed by their power.
Nothing good is on our horizon,
no words to give us courage.
How long will this last,
this torture? How long?
Will you keep your distance forever?
Will you let my illness win?
Why do you hold back your healing?
Why do you withhold your grace?
I know there's a Higher Power;
I recall how you showed your strength.
You drew me aside from my enemies,
you bashed in the heads of my foes.
You made mincemeat of evil forces,
the powers that tried to destroy me.
You loosed the bonds that held me,
the thoughts that steered me wrong.
You brought light to places of darkness
and shrouded the guilt and the shame.
You taught me how to say "no,"
and affirm what is good in my life.
Others may mock your power
and think you do not exist.
Don't waste time on nonbelievers;
stay devoted to those who believe.
Remember the Steps you have taught us,

for the world's full of danger and strife.
Don't let the oppressed remain crushed;
raise up the addicted and shamed.
Get up, God! Make your case
to those who mock your power.
Silence the mouths of the skeptics
who threaten the lives of your people.

PSALM 75

We are grateful to you, our God,
who are always close to us.
We speak of your wondrous works.
At a time that you appoint,
you'll make your just decisions.
When our world is in upheaval
you will keep our foundations firm.
I remind the boastful not to boast,
and the strong not to flaunt their strength:
do not praise yourself with flattery
or speak in public with arrogance.
For nothing on earth can save us,
nor natural power sustain us.
Only you have the power to rescue,
raising the weak and reducing the proud.
You hold a cup of judgment;
you offer us life or death.
Each of us drinks from the cup;
some drain it and then pass away.

But I drink and then I rejoice;
I am grateful to God who saves me.
You break the power of the strong,
and lift up the humble with justice.

PSALM 76

God, you are renowned,
known throughout the world.
You make a dwelling place,
a home among all people.
You heal the disease of addiction—
the feelings and temptations.
You are more majestic
than the highest of mountains.
The brave fall down in awe;
they have no strength to fight.
The arrogant are rebuked;
their power is not enough.
For indeed you are awesome.
Who can stand up to you
once you set your mind?
My Higher Power speaks;
you speak a word of peace.
You offer words of healing
and all the oppressed are saved.
Our anger cannot survive
in the face of your compassion.
I submit my life to you;

you offer me wonderful gifts:

you manage the menacing feelings,

and block the threatening temptations.

PSALM 77

1 I cry out loud for help,

loudly so you can hear me.

2 Whether I'm troubled night or day,

I stretch out my hands to you;

I refuse the comfort of others.

3 I think of you, and I groan;

I consider my plight, and I sigh.

4 I try to keep my eyes open;

I'm so bothered I cannot speak.

5 I remember days past

and years long ago.

6 In the night I reflect on my life;

I meditate and search my heart.

7 Will you always reject me,

never delight in me again?

8 Has your faithfulness disappeared;

are your promises meaningless?

9 Have you forgotten how to be loving?

Have you turned off your compassion?

10 I tell you now: I am grieving

that my Higher Power is gone.

11 I will remember your gracious works,

and the wonders that you have performed.

12 I will ponder your actions
  and reflect on your efforts.

your way

13 The Steps to health are holy;
  what god is as great as you?

14 You are the God who works wonders;
  you have shown your might in our midst.

15 By your strength you have rescued me,
  my descendants reap the reward.

16 Even the oceans know your might;
  the seas tremble in your presence.

17 The storm clouds break open;
  there's thunder and lightning flashes.

18 The wind rushes and the earth shakes.

19 You lead the way through our storms,
  though your footprints remain hidden.

20 You guide us like a shepherd
  filled with concern for your flock.

cf. 104:11-28 ?.

- ? Your way was through the seas, your paths through the great waters.

PSALM 78

Listen to what I have to say;
pay attention to my words.
I will tell you a story,
remind you of a history,
things we've heard before,
passed down through the ages.
We must not hide them from our children;
we must share them with our descendants,
telling the truth about God

and the wonders God has done:
You gave us a Program
and showed us Twelve Steps,
principles to practice ourselves
and hand on to others still suffering,
so they'd learn of your deep caring
and restoring of their sanity.
They don't have to be like their elders
who were stubborn and rebellious,
who did not show their courage
by submitting themselves to you.
They thought they'd save themselves
and needed no other help.
They did not work the Program
nor walk the Twelve-Step path.
They forgot who really healed them,
the miracle of their recovery.
Their families saw that you healed them,
and helped them abstain from X.
God parted the waves in the storm
and gave them a safe passage.
God led them through the darkness
and guided them with the daylight.
He gave them what they needed,
and satisfied deeper desires.
He took away their cravings
and tamped down their temptations.
And yet they turned away

and resumed their abuse of X.
They rebelled against their God,
and tested you with their demands.
They spoke against you, saying,
"Who can heal this dread disease?"
Even though they'd known sobriety
they forgot your awesome power.
We thought this made you angry;
that this would make you rage,
because they did not trust you,
or hope in a Higher Power.
Yet you could not be contained,
and opened up with love:
you rained down generous gifts,
and breathed on them healing grace.
Some addicts received the abundance
of what you created for all.
You who make the wind and rain
generously met their needs.
They received what they had longed for;
they got sober and felt content.
But they did not work the Program,
and lost their lives in the end.
They had not learned the Twelve Steps,
nor accepted your will for their lives,
and so their lives ended early,
an unnecessary loss of life.
Some noticed what had happened;

they looked for you again.

They remembered who once had saved them;

their Higher Power had redeemed them.

They deceived you with their words,

lied to others with their tongues.

They did not work the Program;

their actions were a fraud.

You maintained compassion;

you forgave their sin.

You maintained a patience

that did not resort to rage.

You knew well their weakness,

their limits as mortal beings.

In the desert they often rebelled;

they were wasted and turned from you.

They designed test after test

to see what you would do.

They did not remember your power

when you had healed their disease,

when you had rained down gifts,

and breathed on them healing grace.

Their yearnings led to ailments;

dependencies devoured them.

Consumed by their compulsions,

they were killed by their cravings.

The disease exposed resentments,

let loose their fears and anger.

You did not damp the results:

their illness led to death.
No matter who they were,
their sickness struck them down.
Then you led forth more people,
guiding them through the waste.
You kept them secure in the Steps
while others were swept away.
You brought them to a safe place,
a place of recovery.
You drove out their anxiety
and replaced it with serenity.
Alas, they tested their Higher Power,
and did not work their Program.
They turned faithless like their elders,
and could not admit their wrongs.
Their character defects returned,
and their shortcomings showed their face.
There was no space for you;
they rejected you completely.
They lost their own humility
and replaced it with their pride.
You let them have their way
and then they reaped the ends.
They succumbed to their disease,
and fell to their addictions.
They were consumed by their compulsions,
and relationships ended badly.
People fell to their deaths,

and survivors could not weep.
Then you rose up again,
and shouted, "Enough is enough!"
You drove out the addictions
and swept away the shame.
You did not choose the mighty
as the ones whom you would save.
You chose the poor and powerless;
they are the ones you love.
You make a new abode
among a suffering people.
You select the weak as servants;
you choose them for service.
Their history does not matter;
their admission matters more.
God blesses us with healing,
and skillfully guides our hearts.

PSALM 79

My life is a field of battle;
invaded by a disease,
it's now left in ruins.
My body's no more than a shell
of the life that once I enjoyed.
Now it's empty and useless,
no strength left for me to act.
I've wasted my life on X;
I can no longer care for myself.

I'm now an object of ridicule,

a source of others' delight.

How long will you stay angry, God?

Will you rage like an eternal fire?

Turn it on those who reject you,

toward those who spurn your help.

They're making a mess of their lives

and dragging down family and friends.

Don't cling to the sins of our ancestors.

Extend your tender mercy

because we've fallen so far.

Help us, God! Save us,

because of who you are!

Free us and heal us,

because of who you are.

Why should people say,

"Where is their God?"

Reveal yourself before them

and raise up those who've collapsed.

Hear the groans of the captives;

free those now doomed to die.

Heap your rage on those who ignored you,

sevenfold on those who rejected your help.

Then we who've been healed will praise you,

we'll thank you for a thousand years.

PSALM 80

Listen to us, great Shepherd,
who lead your flock of sheep.
You are the Most High Power
who heal your aching people.
Rouse yourself
and save us!
Restore us, God;
look kindly upon us
and we will be saved.
God of all creation,
how long will you stay angry
and ignore your people's prayers?
We've had our share of tears,
enough to last a lifetime.
We are mocked by our neighbors;
friends laugh at us among themselves.
Restore us, God;
look kindly upon us
and we will be saved.
You knew us when we were just shoots;
you made a space and planted us.
You tilled the soil for us,
and we took root and grew.
We flourished and bore fruit;
others drew life from us;
we matured and strengthened,
and extended ourselves to others.

So why do we stand broken;
why do others steal our fruit?
Ferocious people attack us
and we're ravaged by our disease.
Turn toward us, God, once more,
see how your people suffer;
regard this garden of yours,
planted by your own kind hand.
Some people think they're witty,
and use words to cut us down.
May your word to them do likewise.
Let your kind hand be on us.
May we never turn away from you;
give us life, so that we can thank you.
Restore us, God;
look kindly upon us
and we will be saved.

PSALM 81

Sing out loud to God, our strength,
shout for joy to our Higher Power.
Sing a song, play the drums,
strum the guitar and the harp.
Blow the trumpet; it's a holiday!
It is right to do these things
in order to praise our God.
For a time I did not know you,
and then I found your strength.

You removed the burden I carried;
you answered my cry of distress.
I was tested by my trials;
you rescued me when I called you.
You tell me there's no other god;
I made X the idol of my life.
You alone are the Higher Power
who can free us from captivity.
But we did not listen to you
nor submit our lives to you.
We followed our own stubborn hearts
and thought our own thinking was best.
If only we'd listened to you
and followed the Steps you gave us.
Quickly you would have saved us,
lent your hand to heal our illness.
Those who did not believe
will go to their own doom.
You will satisfy those who trusted,
and nourish them with your great love.

PSALM 82

You come to our meetings;
our Higher Power attends to us.
You ask us, "How long will you wait?
Why do you let your addictions prevail?"
Make things right for addicts;
restore the abuser and the drunk;

rescue the weak and the needy,

and deliver us from the power that grips us,

so that we don't walk around in a daze,

forsaking the knowledge that saves us,

while quaking in the depths of our hearts.

You tell us the glorious truth:

"You are children of the Most High Power."

Yet die we must, like everyone else;

we will fall to the earth and die.

Come on, God!

Tell us the truth,

for all of us belong to you.

PSALM 83

God, do not be silent!

Don't hold your peace or sit still.

Addictions are overwhelming your people.

They are destroying the world you created.

Insidiously they enter our lives;

through subtle treachery they destroy us.

With sinister lies they deceive us,

and ultimately lead us to death.

They promise us what we desire

while they have no power to make it so.

They entice us with false promises.

These are the gods we choose:

alcohol, drugs, and tobacco,

gambling, and food,

porn, and sex,

video games, and the web,

shopping, and shoplifting,

fantasy, and masturbation,

thrills, and exercise,

tattoos and plastic surgery.

Vanquish these enemies of your people;

conquer the power they assert in our world.

Save us addicts and drunks,

gamblers and overeaters,

bulimics and anorexics,

smokers and gamers—

all with compulsive behavior

who have fashioned our own gods.

Be a powerful wind

who blows them away like dust;

burn as a potent fire

who turns them to ash;

chase them down relentlessly

and overcome them with your might.

Let us realize what they really are—

deceptions that lead to death.

Let us see they are only bullies,

and seek only your power at our side.

Let us know that you alone, God,

are the Highest Power in the universe.

PSALM 84

It's good to go to a meeting.
My whole being longs to be there;
maintaining my sobriety demands
that I find my Higher Power there.
Those sober for a minute are welcome,
and those who've abstained for years—
all find a place where they're welcomed,
a place to encounter you.
We delight because you're our strength,
you give us the Steps that lead to health.
As we walk through rough spots
you keep us safe;
you guard us on the path to recovery.
One day at a time we stay sober;
we recognize your presence in our lives.
God of all addicts, hear my prayer,
listen to me, Higher Power.
Behold our God, our shield,
who anoints us with healing.
One hour at a meeting
is better than a thousand elsewhere.
I'd rather have a day of abstinence
than use X for an entire week.
For our Higher Power protects us;
you honor us with new life.
You fulfill the promises made
to those who abstain.

God of addicts,

blessed is everyone who trusts you.

PSALM 85

Lord, you have shown great favor

to those once snared in addictions.

You forgave our guilt,

and pardoned our sins.

You pulled back your rage,

and set aside your anger.

We want to be fully restored;

let go of any displeasure.

Don't stay angry with us forever,

or heap it on our descendants.

Keep on loving us, God,

and give us your salvation.

Let us hear your voice, God,

because you offer us words of peace,

peace for those who trust you.

Your saving grace is at hand

for those who submit to you.

Great things will converge on your people:

love and fidelity will thrive,

justice and peace will come.

You will give us what is good,

and all the world will prosper.

These gifts reveal your presence

as you come into our lives.

PSALM 86

Turn your ear to me and hear me, God,

because I'm in bad shape and need you.

Save my life which is devoted to you;

rescue your servant who trusts you.

You are my God; give me your grace,

because I need your help all day long.

Lift my spirits, my God,

as I offer myself to you.

For you are kind and forgiving,

generous and constant in loving.

Listen to my prayer

and give heed to my request.

When I'm in trouble I turn to you

because I know you will answer me.

There is no other god like you,

nor any deeds that can match yours.

People from all nations have learned

how strong and awesome you are.

You do the most wonderful things

because you alone are God.

I want you to teach me, God,

how to follow the Twelve Steps,

so that I may thrive once more,

and love you with my whole heart.

Your constant love toward me is strong,

you've saved me from my hellish life.

Audacious people make strange claims;

they refuse to believe you are God.

In fact, you're gracious and merciful,

patient and loving and faithful.

Turn toward me with your mercy;

strengthen the one who now seeks you.

Give me a sign that you hear me.

Let others see it and feel ashamed,

as they realize who you are,

for you've given me help and comfort.

PSALM 87

You have given us a Program;

you love those who follow the Steps.

Great things are said about you, God;

at meetings we speak of your grace.

Many know your great might:

we say, "We too are addicts"—

too much booze, drugs, sex, and porn;

we overeat, gamble, and smoke.

At meetings we can admit

we are addicts and need your help.

You've known us from the start,

and how dependent we really were.

But in recovery we say with joy,

"My help comes from you, Higher Power."

PSALM 88

O God, be my salvation!
Day and night I cry out to you.
Let your ears hear my plea;
turn toward me and listen:
My life is filled with troubles,
it's become a living hell.
People don't expect me to live;
they think I won't survive,
that I'm doomed to die a slow death,
that I'll end up dead and forgotten.
They think that you've forgotten me,
and perhaps that's how it seems.
They consign me to a sad fate—
to darkness with no redemption.
I fear you're angry with my failures,
overwhelmed that I've let you down.
Now my companions shun me;
friends are horrified by me.
I'm trapped and cannot escape;
I'm saddened by what I've become.
So daily I cry out to you,
I fall to my knees in prayer.
Don't wait until I'm dead to do something.
If I'm dead, I can never show my thanks.
No one who's dead can praise you,
nor be grateful for what you've done.
No one will hear proclaimed there

the wonderful actions of God.
In fact, I pray to you daily;
each morning I start with prayer.
So why do you set me aside?
Why do you hide from me now?
Since my youth I've suffered this illness;
for years I've been close to death.
It seems you've always been angry,
and determined to end my life.
You come at me from all directions;
there's no place to hide from your rage.
My friends and neighbors shun me;
my family keeps its distance.

PSALM 89

This is the song I will sing:
I'll proclaim your loving-kindness.
I'll declare your love is unending,
and that you are always faithful.
You made an incredible promise,
that you would always be our God;
for us and all our descendants,
you will be God forever.
So let us in recovery praise you,
and speak of your goodness at our meetings.
There's no being that compares to you;
nothing in the heavens is your equal.
You are a Power higher

than any human, angel, or saint.

You have more strength and kindness

than any creature in heaven or on earth.

Who is as mighty as you?

You control the tides of the sea.

You can crush the Leviathan,

any monster on the face of the earth.

Your might reaches all directions:

from the earth to the farthest galaxy,

from the north to the south, the east to the west,

from mountain peaks to the bottom of the sea.

You possess the greatest strength,

rooted in virtue and justice,

in constant love and fidelity.

There are people who shout out joyfully,

who walk steadily in the truth of the Steps.

They praise your wisdom and goodness,

and rejoice in your healing power.

Because our strength is found in yours,

only by your grace are we healed.

Our protection comes from you,

the Highest Power of all.

This is your sacred vision; you say:

"Everyone is crowned with my strength,

I will exalt you among all people.

I find true servants and anoint you;

my healing power strengthens you.

I promise to always be with you,

to stand at your side to save you.
No stupid thinking will outwit you,
nor crazy decisions humble you.
I will crush your temptations
and strike down your obsessions.
I'll be faithful to you with my love
and so your life will be renown.
Wherever you go, I'll be with you.
You will call me 'God' and 'Rock.'
You'll be as privileged as a firstborn,
and as honored as a hero.
I will be constant with my love,
and my promises will stand firm.
My promises will last forever,
to you and all your descendants.
If your children choose a different path
and do not follow my Steps,
if they disobey my teaching
and refuse to follow my path,
then they will feel the results,
and find suffering beyond compare;
but I'll stay constant with my love,
and be faithful to my justice.
I will not break my promises,
or change what I have taught you.
For this is who I am;
I'll never lie to you.
You will keep on having children;

I will not end your families.
They'll last as long as the moon,
as long as the stars can witness."
But we have ignored and rejected you,
and so we can feel your wrath.
You've renounced what you had promised,
and we are left in the dust.
Our man-made barriers are breached;
our so-called strength is in ruins.
Those who are near us just laugh;
neighbors look at us with scorn.
Temptations possess new strength,
cravings return with a vengeance.
It seems you no longer stand with us;
you've turned your back and walked away.
Strength we once had is gone,
belief in ourselves has vanished.
We no longer expect a long life,
and our lives are filled with shame.
How long will you stay hidden?
Will you rage like an eternal fire?
Remember my lifetime is short—
the way you've created all mortals.
None of us can escape death;
all of us must face the end.
Where is the constant love you showed,
the fidelity you promised to all?
Do you see how your servants are teased,

how many of your people are insulted
by the idea that you no longer care?
That is the greatest insult of all.
And still I will thank you
now and forever.

PSALM 90

God, you have been with us here
since the beginning of time.
Before there were mountains or seas,
before there were countless galaxies,
before anything came into being,
there was you.
One day we'll return to dust.
You have no sense of time:
a thousand years is like a day,
or the quick passage of a night.
We mortals are like a dream,
or a flower that blooms for a day;
it flourishes in the morning
and by nighttime it has withered.
We are ravaged by your anger;
we are overwhelmed by your rage.
Our limitations are clear;
our failures are not hidden.
Each of our days is known to you;
our lives fade away like a sigh.
We may live to be seventy,

or eighty years if we're lucky.

Most of them are spent working;

they fly by; and we pass away.

Do we think of the strength of your anger?

Do we remember to hold you in awe?

So teach us to value each day,

in order to gain a wise heart.

Come to us, God, with compassion;

how long will you stay turned away?

Bless us each morning with love,

so our joy will last all day long.

May the number of days of our gladness

be as many as our days of regret.

May your works be evident to all,

and your power to our descendants.

May your favor rest upon us,

and bring us a full recovery.

PSALM 91

We who rely on a Higher Power,

who recover through the power of God,

will know you to be a refuge,

a God in whom we can trust.

For you will free us from our illness,

from captivity to our deadly disease.

With you we find a place of safety,

under your wings we are protected.

You shield us from any danger.

We don't have to fear the night,
nor what comes our way in the day;
neither the temptations that sneak in,
nor the cravings that are obvious.
We see people who don't stay sober,
and others who cannot abstain,
but that doesn't mean we will fall.
It doesn't take much to remember
that our efforts are not in vain.
Because we made you our refuge,
you are our Higher Power.
No longing will be our downfall;
no desire will lead us to fail.
For you will send graces our way,
to guard us each step of the day.
You'll be with us on life's journey,
and mind we don't stumble and fall.
You'll address our heavy problems
and remove our perilous risks.
You will deliver us who love you;
you will protect us who trust you.
When we call to you, you will answer;
you'll rescue us when we're in trouble.
You will give us the gift of long life,
and bless us with peace and recovery.

PSALM 92

It is good to give thanks to you,
and to praise our Higher Power,
to proclaim your love each morning
and your faithfulness every night.
I accompany my prayer with music,
playing the harp and guitar,
because your healing makes me happy;
what you've done for me makes me sing.
Your works are so great,
and your thinking is profound.
We're slow to understand;
some people just don't get it:
addictions can spring up quickly,
and then flourish for years.
Yet they are also deadly,
while you, God, live forever.
Those who do not change will die;
their illness will be the death of them.
Yet we have been given a gift;
we've been anointed with recovery.
We've seen our friends hit bottom,
and never find a way to get better.
The sober will flourish like bamboo,
and grow like giant redwoods.
They thrive in their closeness to you;
they prosper by enacting your will.
For decades their recovery bears fruit;

they carry the message to others.
They practice the principles daily,
and show your goodness to all.

PSALM 93

God reigns, wrapped in majesty;
Our Higher Power is mighty.
God has made the universe,
God rules over all, forever.
Unrest has died down;
chaos has been conquered.
Confusion has been vanquished;
disorder has disappeared.
The Steps are right for me;
they guide me to serenity
with you, forever.

PSALM 94

Stand up, God of healing!
Come forth to offer treatment.
Rise up, God of health!
Cure those who need you.
How long must we remain ill
before you help us recover?
Alas, some of us are proud;
we boast that we need no help.
We harm those who love us,
and afflict the innocent.

So we die and make widows;
our children lose their parents.
Then we blame you as the cause,
and claim that you did nothing.
How can we be so stupid?
How can we be such fools?
You make ears, but cannot hear?
You make eyes, but cannot see?
You are most wise, but cannot think?
While human thoughts are just air.
Blessed are those who learn discipline,
the lessons of self-control.
They recover from their illness
while others fall into a pit.
You do not leave us in our pain,
nor forget the addicts' suffering.
You offer a healing process;
healing is found through the Steps.
Who protects me from temptation?
Who strengthens me when I crave?
It is you who gives me help;
without you I'd be dead.
When I'm about to slip,
you're there to hold me up.
When my thoughts weigh me down,
your wisdom lifts me up.
Unhealthy plans are not yours;
you never plot to cause harm.

My illness is at fault,

and leads innocents to death.

But you've become my strength,

the refuge for my life.

You come to wipe out illness,

and restore addicts to health.

PSALM 95

Let us sing a song to our God;

a joyful hymn of praise.

We come to you with thanksgiving,

singing a song of praise.

For you, our God, are great,

no other Power is more.

Your strength fills all creation;

the universe is your handiwork.

We shall worship and bow down

and kneel to the God who saves us.

We are the people you lead;

our recovery comes from you.

Each day we listen for your voice.

We do not want hard hearts

as we had when we were ill,

when we tested, and made demands,

although we knew of your might.

You held back your healing love

for our hearts had gone astray.

We found other gods for ourselves

and did not follow your ways.

And so without you and your truth

we spent years of our lives without rest.

PSALM 96 — *addictions = idolatry*

1 It's time to sing a new song,

  a hymn to God round the world.

2 We bless your power, O God,

  who rescues us every day.

3 Let's tell the whole world our story, *"all the peoples*

  your works among the addicted.

4 For great is our mighty God,

  the Highest Power of all. *"gods of the peoples"*

5 We made X to be our idol

  yet the power of X is small.

6 You are strength and beauty;

  you are love and power. *honor! glory and strength*

7 Give credit where credit is due:

  you are the one who can heal.

You are the Highest Power;

we're grateful for what you have done.

We attribute the goodness to you,

and hold you in awe round the world.

Let's tell all people of your strength—

our sobriety that you maintain,

because you are justice and love.

11 Let the heavens and earth be glad;

  let the seas and the lands rejoice;

let plants and animals sing

because you are alive and well.

13 Now you have come to heal us,

to restore the addicted among us.

You will act with compassion

and guide us with the truth.

to judge the earth

He will judge the world
with righteousness, and
the peoples with truth,

PSALM 97

1 God reigns!

Let the earth rejoice

and the islands, too.

2 You are present in our storms;

when fog or darkness surround us,

you, though unseen, are still here.

When we crave and burn with desire,

you offer us gifts of grace.

When fears come all of a sudden,

you offer the gift of peace.

When everything's falling apart,

you remain a firm foundation.

The universe proclaims your goodness,

people need only look to see it.

Yet we addicts choose other gods;

we make false idols of X,

as if they have any power!

8 Addicts hear some good news:

there's a way out of their mess,

because of your healing power.

You are a Higher Power,

even greater than X.

You love those who abstain.

You guard us from temptation,

and rescue us from our longing.

Light emerges for addicts

and joy for those recovering.

We thank you, God, for healing,

and are grateful for your compassion.

PSALM 98

Stand together and sing to God

who has done some wonderful things!

You have reached out with your strength

and helped the addicted to recover.

You are the source of recovery;

in the sight of all you bring healing.

You maintain your love and compassion;

the whole world affirms your goodness.

So make some joy-filled noise,

and sing to your heart's content!

Blast the brass and pluck the string;

blow the winds and pound the drums.

Make some joy-filled noise!

Let the fish of the sea

and the creatures on land,

the waters of the earth

and the mountains above

all sing to you, God, who heals.
For you have shown us compassion
and saved us by your love.

PSALM 99

You rule! We're in awe;
you're a Power with no rival.
You are filled with might;
there is no greater god.
We praise your greatness,
for you are awesome.
Higher Power, source of justice,
you have come with healing;
you bring recovery to the weak,
and abstinence to the addict.
So we fall to our knees and give thanks;
we humbly bow down in our gratitude.
We have friends whose lives are better;
acquaintances whose lives have improved.
They called out to you and were heard;
they learned the Steps and followed them.
They practiced the principles daily,
and submitted themselves to your will.
God, you answered their prayers;
you showed them tender mercy
while they made amends for their wrongs.
We are grateful to you, our God.
We praise your goodness each day
for you, our God, are healing.

PSALM 100

Let the whole world make some noise!

Now is the time to show gratitude,

and to make beautiful music for God,

because you are our Higher Power,

the one who made us, to whom we belong.

We are part of your own family.

We're glad to be in your presence,

who's around and beyond and within.

We are grateful for what we've received.

Beyond doubt our Higher Power's good;

your love for us will last for all time;

you will be faithful for all ages.

PSALM 101

My God, you are loving and just;

I state this clearly for the record:

I will study the Twelve Steps;

for recovery is a path to life.

I will strive for integrity

in my personal life.

I will not let myself be distracted

by temptations that pass before me.

I am sad for those who walk away,

but I won't follow their lead.

I won't let my heart be diverted;

I'll do my best to avoid false gods.

Some of my friends have been skeptical;

I hope I can show them I'm real.
I don't want to be a cynic;
I want only to keep my abstinence.
I will walk alongside other addicts,
so that together we can stay sober.
We can learn from one another,
and together we can make it.
Those who deceive make it harder—
on themselves and those around them.
Those who lie only fool themselves;
no one believes them or their words.
One day at a time I will live;
each day I promise to stay sober.
I will avoid getting close to temptation
and the people who expect me to fail.

PSALM 102

Hear my prayer, Higher Power;
may my cry reach your ears.
Do not hide from me
in this time of distress.
Turn your ears toward me,
and respond to me quickly.
My days are empty like smoke;
my body is burning up.
My heart is worn out;
I'm too tired to eat.
I groan out loud in pain;

my skin has turned to flab.
I'm a soul lost in the desert,
a child lost in the wilderness.
I'm awake through the night,
and all alone.
People tease me through the day,
and my name has become a joke.
My food tastes like ashes
and my tears are my drink.
I know you're angry at me
and have cast me aside.
The days slip away like shadows
as I turn into skin and bones.
You, my God, are seated on high;
your power will last forever.
I know you'll show me compassion,
because that's who you really are.
I want to keep my life,
and be kind to myself as well.
All people will learn to honor you,
and the powers that be will respect you.
You will restore my health
and everyone will know it's you.
You will hear the cry of the despondent
and not despise our prayers.
Future generations will remember this;
one day the unborn will hear this;
that a Higher Power listened

and heard the groans of the addicted.

And so you'll be acclaimed
and praised the world over;
when people gather, they'll praise you,
and nations will honor your power.

My strength gave out in midlife;
I thought my life was over.
I pleaded with you not to die
while I yearned for a longer life.

Long ago you created this world,
and the fullness of the universe.
They will pass, but you will not;
clothing wears thin; but you prevail.
Our children will survive
and their children will live with you.

PSALM 103

I am grateful to you, God;
with my whole being I thank you.
I am grateful to you
and will never forget what you have given me.

For it is you who have healed me,
have healed every one of my troubles.
You have rescued my life from the grave.
You crowned me with loving-kindness.
You have filled my life with good things,
and revived me with new strength.
You have made things right again,

and given sobriety to me who was addicted.
You have made your ways known to the lost
and revealed your power to the hopeless.
You are compassion and love,
slow to anger and rich in kindness.
Your anger does not last;
soon enough it comes to an end.
You do not treat me the way my behavior deserves,
and you do not punish me because of my addiction.
For as high as the heavens are above the earth,
so great is your power to overcome our disease.
As far as the east is from the west
are you able to push away our addiction.
Like a compassionate parent toward a child,
you have empathy for us addicts.
For you know our human limitations,
and you're always aware of our helplessness.
Our human lifetimes are short;
we blossom and then fade away.
When the wind blows we're scattered,
then we die and are not seen again.
But you, Higher Power, are eternal
for those who count on you.
Your healing power prevails
from generation to generation
when we turn to you for help,
when we rely on you for our strength.
God, you make your home in heaven

while your power is accessible to all.

All in recovery, be grateful to God

who is mighty in power, who keeps all promises.

Pay attention to God's great wisdom.

Be grateful to God, all who are recovering

as you struggle to keep your sobriety.

Be grateful to God, all who seek healing,

for your Higher Power is always with you.

My whole being, be grateful to God!

PSALM 104

1) I am grateful to you, God;

my Higher Power, you're great!

Your whole being is wonderful;

2) you shine like a glowing lamp.

3 Your power lights up the heavens

and your strength calms the seas;

your might spans height and depth,

4 your force reaches left and right;

your might guides the winds,

while fire reveals your passion.

5 You set ~~me~~ on firm ground *— the earth (NRSV) — it's foundations*   *["me" replaces "the earth"]*

so that I will not be shaken.

6 You wrap me in a protective garment

so I will not be harmed.   *— "the waters"?*   *Turning creation into a threat*

7 What threatens me runs away,

and all temptations flee.

8–9 They quit my life and depart;

you drive them out for good.

10 New life springs up;

it shows all over.

I am a source of life for others; *(your are)*

they learn from me and thrive.

Some draw close to learn;

they grow and are glad.

But all this comes from you;

all this healing is your work:

I awaken from my numbness

and see the beauty around me.

I feel new freedom and happiness,

while I do not regret my past.

I feel serenity and live in peace.

What I have learned assists those around me;

I am unselfish and concerned about others;

my self-pity and uselessness are gone.

My fear of people and poverty has disappeared;

I can respond to things that once baffled me.

I realize that you're doing for me

what I could not do for myself.

I don't fight with anyone or anything;

I react sanely and normally!

My avoidance of X is effortless.

I am safe and protected.

My problem has been removed.

I'm neither boastful nor afraid.

I wait for you to give what I need;

"I" replaces "You" (=God)!

vv 11–28 ??

creation?

for what I receive I am grateful.

You show me generous love,

and my life is filled with goodness.

When I can't find you, I'm aghast.

29 If you stopped loving me, I'd die. ⌐ (vs. 29 ?)

30 Your spirit keeps me alive and well;

you renew me from the ground up.

31 May your renown last forever;

may you be pleased in what you've done.

32 Look around and see what you've accomplished;

you leave a mark on everything good.

33 So I open my mouth to sing;

I'll sing as long as I live.

34 May these thoughts be pleasing to you

for I'm glad that you're my God.

35 May all addictions be destroyed

and healing take their place.

Make it so, God; make it so.

PSALM 105

I'm grateful, God; and I tell others

what great things you've done.

I sing your praises

and speak of your deeds.

May others know them as well;

may their hearts swell with joy.

We seek the strength of our God,

to live safely under your protection.

We remember what you have done—
great deeds and healing for your people.
For you are the Higher Power,
more than anything else on earth.
You remember your great promises
and remain faithful to your word.
You do not skip a generation;
you keep your word to all nations.
If there were just a few of us,
you'd still be true to your word.
No one could stand in your way;
no one is greater than you.
When we were at a low point,
you acted on our behalf.
You brought people into our lives
who could show us another way.
When we were enslaved to X
and held captive in its snare,
you kept your enduring promise
and sent the help we needed.
People in recovery taught us;
they showed us a different path.
They listened to us without judgment;
they understood what others did not.
You showed us a new land;
Twelve Steps would take us there.
Promises were made and kept;
we were amazed that they bore fruit.

You gave us sponsors who cared;
they showed us what we couldn't see.
They laughed and cried with us;
they told us the truth when it hurt.
We tried to do things on our own;
that didn't go so well.
We rebelled and said, "No more!"
We tried other paths, and failed.
We felt attacked from within,
and remembered enemies of the past.
We resented what had happened
and who had done us wrong.
We clung to anger and fear
as if they could rescue us.
We lost some friends and family;
we clung to X as our savior.
We finally found a way
to walk away from X.
What a relief we felt!
Not as bad as expected.
We asked for help and you heard us;
we surrendered, and you jumped right in!
We had known emptiness, and were filled.
What once was paltry became abundance.
You remember your promise and your people.
You rescue us from slavery
and pull our lives out of the grave.
You give us Twelve Steps

that will keep us alive.

Oh, yes!

PSALM 106

1 We praise you, and we thank you,
   for your love is steady and true.

2 Who else can do what you do?

3 We reap the benefits
   when we act justly and stay abstinent.

4 Don't lose sight of me
   as you care for all people;
   may all of us see your goodness
   and enjoy the fruits of your healing.

   I and my ancestors became addicts;
   we succumbed to our disease
   and caused pain and harm to others.

   We forgot your goodness and strength,
   your desire to keep us safe;
   we rebelled against your power.

8 Even then you reached out
   and saved us from drowning;
   you rescued us from floodwaters.

   For we had not sought your wisdom,
   nor relied upon your power;
   we clung to our obsessive thoughts.

   As we carefully search our lives,
   we make a fearless inventory
   and admit our wrongs and defects:

we hold onto our resentments;
we replay and relive the pain,
and become a swamp of self-pity.
We nurture our hurt and anger,
we stuff it, then let it explode;
we blame others for what we've done.
We won't let go of our fears;
we let them become gigantic;
then they misguide our actions.
Sex has been a problem;
selfishness has hurt me
and damaged others too.
My self-esteem is shot;
I'm filled with shame and remorse,
and think that no one cares.
I'm also filled with pride,
and humility that's a lie;
ambition makes poor decisions.
My relationships are a mess;
I don't respect my commitments;
I go where I don't belong.
I long for real security;
I try to find it with more stuff,
I think money will solve my problems.
I yearn for personal safety;
yet I put myself in danger.
I keep my distance to avoid pain.
I am selfish, and dishonest, and

inconsiderate to myself and others.

I have way too many defects.

You've delivered me many times.

You've set me free to start anew;

yet I rebelled and turned away.

You see my distress and try once more.

You recall your love and show compassion;

seeing our captivity, your heart breaks.

I admit my wrongs to you;

I honestly confess these faults.

I ask for your forgiveness.

I admit my wrongs to another,

and tell them all my faults.

They listen without judgment.

47 You save us, God, from our disease,

so we give thanks to you.

We live one day at a time.

48 Thanks be to you, Higher Power,

through every generation!

Let it be so, today and forever.

PSALM 107

God, we are grateful to you,

for your goodness lasts forever.

Those you have rescued should say so:

those whose lives you saved

and brought in from the cold,

from east and west, from north and south.

Some of us were lost in a wasteland,
we couldn't find our way home;
we were hungry and thirsty
and wracked by our disease.
We were in trouble and cried out;
you set us free from distress.
You showed us a straight path;
you led us to recovery.
May our hearts be thankful
for all your wonderful deeds.
You have quenched our hungers,
and satisfied our thirsts.
For some time we sat in darkness,
prisoners of misery and gloom.
We rebelled against your ways,
and snubbed our Higher Power.
Our hearts were heavy and burdened;
they broke with anguish and sadness.
We were in trouble and cried out;
you set us free from distress.
Prisoners of misery and gloom,
you set us captives free.
God, we are grateful to you;
your goodness lasts forever.
Your love is strong and wonderful;
it knocks down walls that imprison us.
Some were sick and tired
of being sick and tired.

We abhorred our lives;

we were close to death.

We were in trouble and cried out;

you set us free from distress.

You spoke a word of healing

and saved our lives from destruction.

God, we are grateful to you;

your goodness lasts forever.

Now we amend our lives

and tell others what you have done.

Some of us were tossed about

on waves of chaos and stress.

We had our highs and lows;

we hardly knew what end was up.

The storms of life arose;

we were thrown around like rag dolls.

We lost our courage and hope

as calamities overwhelmed us.

We were in trouble and cried out;

you set us free from distress.

You stilled the storms and hushed the waves;

they quieted down and you brought us to shore.

God, we are grateful to you;

your goodness lasts forever.

We share our stories with others,

and tell our good news in groups.

Our choices can turn good things to bad,

and blessings into curses.

A juicy fruit can turn rotten
because of poor decisions.
But you can turn the bad to good,
and a curse into a blessing.
You can fill the empty ones,
and turn survival into thriving.
With your help and our efforts,
recovery takes root in us.
Blessings multiply greatly,
and prosperity blossoms.
When we were brought down
by addiction and sorrow,
we got lost in our obsession;
our aim was "one more X."
You saw our greater need
and steered us to safety.
Now we know what you have done;
skeptics have to shut their mouths!
May all people have the wisdom
to remember your eternal love.

PSALM 108

My heart is steadfast, God,
as I take one day at a time.
I will make music and sing,
as my whole being awakes.
Wake up, guitar and harp;
wake up, sleepy world!

I'll express my gratitude to you,
and speak about your love to the nations.
Your steadfast love is powerful,
and your fidelity lasts forever.
My Higher Power is mighty,
its strength can heal the whole earth.
May the heavens and earth
be filled with praise for you.
Conquer my addiction by your power;
come to the rescue of those whom you love.
My joyful God has promised healing:
"I'll give you hope and perseverance,
honesty, faith, and forgiveness.
Abstinence is yours;
serenity is my gift.
I'll drive out fear, wash away anger,
and triumph over resentments."
Who will lead me to a safe place?
Who can manage my feelings?
Have you rejected me, God?
Have you abandoned me to my disease?
Give me your healing for this illness,
because all human aid is worthless.
With you I shall succeed,
for only you have the power.

PSALM 109

1 God, don't be so quiet!

2 [This illness] is picking on me *"They..."*
   and assaulting me with its lies.

3 [It] has no reason to attack me
   and hurl its hurtful words.

4 [This illness] prods self-accusal
   even as I pray for relief.

5 [The disease] returns evil for good
   and hatred when I love.

6-7 It conspires to bring false witness
   so my innocence will be called "guilt."

8 Its goal is to knock me down
   and shorten my life.

9 My spouse will be widowed
   and my children will be orphans.

10 They'll have to resort to begging
   and their home will fall to ruin.

11 The mortgage will go unpaid
   and strangers will get the property.
   No one will show me kindness,
   nor compassion to my children.
   My lineage will disappear,
   and my name will be forgotten.
   They'll claim my father was evil,
   and destroy my mother's name.
   Will God remember my family thus
   as others damage their reputation?

People say I mistreated others
and hounded people to death.
They say that I cursed, so now they curse me;
that I withheld blessings, and they do the same.
They claim the punishment fits my crime:
that I am steeped in sin,
and so must be condemned,
reminded each day of my fall.
May the same thing happen to them
for the evil they've done to me!
Now, God, take up my cause
and deliver me because of your love.
For I'm the one who is poor;
in fact, my heart is broken.
I'm a shadow of my former self
who can be brushed aside like a bug.
This disease has wrecked my body;
I'm wasting away with weakness.
I've become an object of scorn,
someone easy to make fun of.
Help me, Higher Power!
Save me by your love.
Let everyone know it's you,
and nothing I've done on my own.
Even when they curse, you bless;
They shame themselves (and I like it).
They bring it on themselves;
they wrap themselves in guilt.

One day I'll stand in crowds
and proclaim your mighty goodness.
For you will stand by my side
and save me from this disease.

PSALM 110

God, you're always near at hand:
"Stick with me and I'll take care of you."
Higher Power, you're ready
to hold sway in our lives.
We must surrender to you,
wholeheartedly let you lead.
Within your powerful reign
we will follow your will.
You'll always keep your promises;
You are God forever.
God, you stand with me;
you will conquer my defects.
You will crush my shortcomings,
and shatter my addiction.
You will celebrate my success
when I raise my head in victory.

PSALM 111

Thank you, God!
My heart is filled with thanks
when I gather with others at meetings.
We marvel at your great deeds

when we study the Big Book.
You honor us with healing;
your mercy has no end.
You are well known by us
for being our saving strength.
You fulfill your promises
and give us sobriety;
you renew our lives
and grant us serenity.
Your words are worthy of trust;
the Steps are right and true.
They lead to effective living
and personal satisfaction.
We've had a spiritual awakening
and carry this message to others.
We practice the principles daily;
they are wisdom to guide our lives.
Turning to you is the Second Step,
trusting in you is the Third.

PSALM 112

Thank you, God!

1 Blessed are those who hope in you,
who delight in following the Steps. — *his commandments*

2 Their descendants reap the benefits
of growing up in healthy homes.

3 They prosper in their endeavors,
and their goodness fills the land.

4 In recovery they shine in the darkness,
  they are merciful, gracious, and just.
5 They do well who are generous in giving
  and conduct their business with justice.
6 Their goodness will not be forgotten;
  they will be remembered forever.
7 They aren't afraid of bad news,
  because their hearts are strengthened by you.
8 They walk steadily and unafraid,
  and look their opponents in the eye.
9 They give freely to those in need;
  their virtues and goodness are honored.
10 The wicked see this and get angry;
  they sputter, and nothing more.

PSALM 113

Thank you, God!
We in recovery thank you;
we'll be grateful all our lives.
We'll sing your praise
today and forever.
From the east to the west
we'll shout your praise,
because our Higher Power
is so very very strong!
There is no other power
as strong as our Higher Power!
He rescues us from our hell holes,

and raises us from the pits.
We find a seat at meetings
next to CEOs and clergy,
with seniors and with teens,
with parents, and homeless, too.
Thank you, God!

PSALM 114

As I started to recover,
and left behind my addiction,
I began a new way of living,
and you became my shelter.
People got out of my way;
they knew something was different.
There was a new bounce in my step,
my outlook on life had changed.
Why did they move away?
Were they afraid that I was different?
Was the bounce in my step a threat?
Was my new outlook a challenge?
You are alive and active here;
I shake in my shoes in your presence.
You can save the dying addicts
and make us healthy again.

PSALM 115

We don't deserve an honor,
because recovery is your doing;

it flows from your loving-kindness.

No one dares say, "There is no God."

Our Higher Power is mighty,

and does what brings delight.

Other gods are wood and metal,

with eyes that can't see,

and ears that can't hear,

with noses that can't smell

and mouths that can't speak.

We ourselves made idols

of X, and Y, and Z;

they could not fill our needs

or take away our pain.

All false gods are futile;

to trust them is futile too.

Addicts, put your trust in God.

God is a help and a shield.

Put your faith in a Higher Power,

who is a help and a shield.

All who seek recovery, trust God

who is a help and a shield.

You do not forget; you love us.

You love the addicted;

you love the recovering.

You love those looking for hope,

no matter when we show up.

All power belongs to you,

which you share with us mortal beings.

The dead offer no praise;

the buried sleep in silence.

But we in recovery praise you

today and forevermore.

It's true!

PSALM 116

I love my Higher Power,

who hears my cries and prayers.

You turn your ear toward me,

so I'll pray as long as I live.

The snare of death surrounded me;

hell had me in its grip;

I suffered alone and in pain.

Then I called to you for help:

"If you hear me, save my life!"

You give us grace; act justly;

and show us loving-kindness.

You protect the simple ones:

at my lowest, you saved me.

Now my body can rest in peace

because you've been generous to me.

You have delivered me from death,

saved me from stumbling and tears.

I live each day in your presence,

striving to follow your will.

When afflicted, I kept some faith,

while others told lies about me.

What can I do for you
after all you've done for me?
I will worship you every day,
and think about you each night.
I will keep my promise to you
and abstain each day from X.
Even on my deathbed I'll think of you.
I'll surrender to you with my last breath.
I will serve you and serve others
because you freed me from the noose.
I will carry this message to others,
and put it into practice.
I will keep my promise to you
and continue to abstain each day.
At meetings I'll share my hope;
I'll support my fellow addicts.
Thank you, God!

PSALM 117

We praise you, God!
We praise our Higher Power!
For your loving-kindness is strong,
and your fidelity lasts forever.
Yes, it's true!

PSALM 118

Give thanks to God, who's always good,
for God's healing lasts forever.

Let the addicted say,

"God's healing lasts forever."

Let those in recovery say,

"God's healing lasts forever."

Let all who look for hope say,

"God's healing lasts forever."

In my great distress I called out;

You answered me and gave me space.

I have no fear because you are at my side;

how could anyone threaten my sobriety?

My Higher Power's on *my* side,

so I can handle what comes my way.

It's better to trust you than humans;

it's better than the powers that be.

Surrounded by temptations, I turned my back;

they came at me from all directions,

and with your strength I cut them off.

They attacked me like a swarm of bees;

they flashed at me like a blazing fire.

With your strength I fought them off.

They pushed me hard, and I was falling,

and then you rushed to my aid.

You are my strength and my grace;

my Higher Power saves me.

At meetings I share my story:

"God has shown great power;

God has done great things."

I will not die! I will live,

and tell others what you have done.
I had suffered greatly,
but you didn't let me die.
Open the doors for the rescued,
so I can go in and give thanks.
The Steps are doors to you, God;
addicts can enter and find peace.
I am grateful that you responded;
you have been my salvation.
The one who seemed hopelessly lost
has become a banquet centerpiece.
This is all your doing,
and it's great to see it happen.
Today is a day you will act,
so let's all of us be joyful.
The one who recovers is blessed,
and becomes a blessing for others.
You are our Higher Power,
and have given us a light.
Prepare the hall for a feast,
and set the table with flowers,
because today I honor you, God;
I praise my Higher Power.
Give thanks to God, who's always good,
for God's healing lasts forever.

PSALM 119

An alphabetical collection of wisdom sayings from Anonymous Groups

A

Abstinence is the first thing in my life, without exceptions.

Accept your admission and get a new attitude.

Act as if . . .

Addicts heal from the outside in . . . but feel from the inside out.

Addiction is an equal opportunity destroyer.

Although we are not responsible for our disease, we are responsible for our recovery.

An addict alone is in bad company.

An addict cannot be grateful and hateful at the same time.

Answer is abstinence.

B

Be as enthusiastic about recovery as you were about your addiction.

Be careful what you pray for; you're liable to get it.

Be part of the solution, not part of the problem.

Before engaging your mouth, put your mind in gear!

Before you say "I can't," say "I'll try."

Bend your knees before you bend your elbows.

The best things in life aren't things.

Better is enough.

Bring the body and the mind will follow.

But for the grace of God.

C

Call your sponsor before, not after, you take the first drink.

Change is a process, not an event.

"Coincidence" is a miracle in which God chooses to remain anonymous.

Count your blessings.

Courage to change.

Cultivate an attitude of gratitude.

D

Depression is anger turned inward.

The disease is physical. The cause is emotional. The cure is spiritual.

Do it sober.

Do the next "right thing."

Don't compare your inside with someone else's outside.

Don't quit five minutes before the miracle happens.

Don't pick up; ask for help, call your sponsor, and go to meetings.

Don't use, no matter what.

Don't hurry. Don't worry. Don't compare.

E

Easy does it.

Easy does it, but do it.

EGO = Easing God Out.

The elevator is broken. Use the Steps.

Every day is a gift. That is why we call it the "present."

Examine your motives.

Expectations are premeditated resentments.

F

Faith is not belief without proof, but trust without reservation.

Failure is success on the installment plan, if I learn from it.

Fake it 'til you make it.

Feel it, don't fill it.

Feeling brings healing.

Feelings are not facts.

The First Step is the only Step a person has to work perfectly.

The flip side to forgiveness is resentment.

Forgiveness is letting go of a better past.

Formula for failure: try to please everyone.

G

Get it; give it; grow in it.

Give time time.

GOD = Good Orderly Direction.

God doesn't make junk.

God taught us to laugh again; but God, please don't let us forget that we once cried.

Growing old is mandatory; growing up is optional.

H

Half measures avail us nothing.

HALT = don't get too Hungry, Angry, Lonely, Tired.

Have a good day, unless of course you have made other plans.

Help is only a phone call away.

HOPE = Happy Our Program Exists.

Hope is the risk that must be run.

How does it work? It works just fine.

How important is it?

HOW it works = Honesty, Open-mindedness, and
    Willingness.

Hugs, not drugs.

Humility is not thinking less of yourself, but thinking of
    yourself less.

Humility is our acceptance of ourselves.

I

I can expect only to get better at this, not control it.

I can't. God can. I think I'll let God.

I never let go of anything that didn't have my claw marks
    all over it.

I won't starve to death between meals.

If I think, I won't drink. If I drink, I can't think.

If it is meant to be, I can't stop it.

If it isn't God's will, I can't make it happen.

If not this, then something better.

If you are not progressing in recovery, you are going
    backwards.

If you can be humble, you'll learn faster.

If you do what you always did, you'll get what you always
    got.

If you don't want to slip, stay away from slippery places.

If you expect respect, be the first to show some.

If you fail to plan, you plan to fail.

If you find a path with no obstacles, it probably doesn't lead
    anywhere.

If you have one foot in yesterday and one foot in tomorrow, you'll pee all over today.

If you like everyone you've met in your group, then you haven't been to enough meetings.

If you sit in the barber's chair long enough, you'll eventually get a haircut.

If you turn it over and don't let go of it, you will be upside down.

If you want to stay clean, don't use.

Is your Program powered by willpower or Higher Power?

It is not the experience of today that drives people mad; it is the remorse or bitterness for something which happened yesterday and the dread of what tomorrow may bring.

It is possible to change without improving; it is impossible to improve without change.

It isn't the load that weighs us down, it's the way we carry it.

It takes time to get better.

It's a pity we can't forget our troubles the same way we forget our blessings.

It's a simple Program for complicated people.

It's about X until it's not about X.

It's not what you're eating; it's what's eating you.

J

Journeys of a thousand miles begin with the First Step.

Just for today.

K

Keep an open mind.

Keep coming back.

Keep coming back; it works if you work it.

Keep it simple.

Keep your recovery first if you want it to last.

The key to freedom is in the Steps.

L

Learn to listen and listen to learn.

The lesson I must learn is simply that my control is limited to my own behavior, my own attitudes.

Let it begin with me.

Listen and learn.

Live and let live.

Live in the now.

Live life on life's terms.

Look after the little things.

Look for your Higher Power in all things.

Look for similarities rather than differences.

M

Many meetings, many chances; few meetings, few chances; no meetings, no chances.

Meeting makers make it.

Minds are like parachutes: they won't work unless they're open.

Misery is optional.

More will be revealed.

Most things can be preserved in alcohol; dignity, however, is not one of them.

My Higher Power is whatever I turn to in a crisis.

N

The newcomer is the most important person in any meeting.

Nothing is so bad that using won't make worse.

The only thing you have to change is everything.

O

One addict talking to another.

One day at a time.

One drink is too many and a thousand not enough.

P

Pain is the touchstone of spiritual progress.

Pass it on.

People who don't go to meetings don't hear about what happens to people who don't go to meetings.

Practice an attitude of gratitude.

Principles before personalities.

Progress, not perfection.

Q

Quit taking it personally.

R

Recovery begins with the First Step.

Recovery doesn't happen overnight.

Recovery is a journey, not a destination.

Recovery is an education without a graduation.

Religion is for those who fear God. Spirituality is for those who have been to hell and back.

Remember that addiction is incurable, progressive, and
   fatal. It takes time to get better.

Repetition is nature's only form of permanence.

Resentment is like drinking poison and expecting someone
   else to die.

The road to disappointment is paved with expectation.

The road to sobriety is a simple journey for confused people
   with a complicated disease.

S

Seven days without a meeting makes one weak.

Share your happiness.

Share your pain.

Sick and tired of being sick and tired.

SLIP = Sobriety Lost Its Priority.

Slogans are wisdom written in shorthand.

Sober up and tighten up (financially).

Sobriety delivers everything that X promised.

Sobriety is a journey, not a destination.

Some of us are sicker than others.

The sooner I surrender, the better.

Sorrow is looking back; worry is looking around.

Spirituality is the ability to get our minds off ourselves.

Sponsors carry the message, not the person.

Stay sober for yourself.

Stick with the winners.

Suit up and show up.

T

Take the cotton out of your ears and put it in your mouth.

Take what you can use and leave the rest.

Take what you need and leave the rest.

Take what you like and leave the rest.

There are none too dumb for a Twelve-Step program, but many are too smart.

There are two days in every week which we have no control over: yesterday and tomorrow.

Today is the only day we can change.

There is no magic in recovery, only miracles.

There is no situation that a compulsive act can't make worse.

This too shall pass.

Thoughts are just thoughts. You don't have to act.

Time takes time.

Time wasted in getting even can never be used in getting ahead.

To be forgiven, we must forgive.

To keep it (recovery), you have to give it away.

To keep what you have, you have to give it away.

To thine own self be true.

Together we can make it.

Try not to place conditions on your sobriety.

Trying is dying.

Trying to pray is praying.

Turn it over.

Turn it over, don't turn it off.

The Twelve Steps are not for those who want them, but for those who need them.

The Twelve Steps: trust God, clean house, help others, pray.

The two ways to learn are the hard way, and the harder way.

U

Usually I'm wrong anyway; and even when I'm right,
    it's not forever.

W

The way to ask for help is to say, "I need help."

We are not human beings having spiritual experiences;
    we are spiritual beings having human experiences.

We are only as sick as our secrets.

We'll love you until you learn to love yourself.

We're all here because we're not all there.

We're responsible for the effort, not the outcome!

What goes around, comes around.

What other people think of me is none of my business.

Whatever you put before your recovery, you will surely lose.

When people try to control their addiction, they have
    already lost control.

When all else fails, follow directions.

When wallowing in your self-pity, get off the cross! We need
    the wood.

When your head begins to swell, your mind stops growing.

Wherever you go, there you are.

Willing to go to any lengths.

Willingness is the key.

Worry prevents recovery.

Would you rather be right or happy?

X

X is not my friend. I have plenty of other friends and interests.

X is whatever I turn to when I'm in distress; I think X is my Higher Power.

X is whatever tempts me or threatens my abstinence or serenity.

Y

Yesterday is history; tomorrow is mystery; stay in today.

You are exactly where God wants you to be.

You are never too late unless you miss the Closing.

You are not alone.

You are not required to like it; you're only required to do it.

You can only keep what you have by giving it away.

You can't do it alone, but only you can do it.

You can't think your way into a new way of living; you have to live your way into a new way of thinking.

You only get out of it what you put into it.

You received without cost; now give without charge.

You will be amazed.

Your Twelve-Step program will work if you want it to work.

Your worth should never depend on another person's opinion.

PSALM 120

God, I call to you and you answer me
when I am in trouble.
Save me from stinkin' thinkin'
and the deceptions of my disease.
What will I gain from
listening to lies—
harmful words that fill my mind
and pierce my heart?
I am a wretched soul,
surrounded by addicts
as sick as I am.
I've spent too much time
with people like myself.
Even when I try to recover
they pull me back.

PSALM 121

I turn my eyes to the skies and ask,
"Where does my help come from?"
My help comes from a Higher Power,
a power greater than myself.
God will not allow my foot to slip,
for God never sleeps a wink.
It's true that God never naps;
God tracks my every step.
God is the protector at my side,
who gives me shade from the sun

and moonlight through the night.
God protects me from every temptation
in order to preserve my life.
God safeguards my comings and goings
all the days of my life.

PSALM 122

I rejoiced when they said to me,
"Let's go get treatment."
Now at last
I've found sobriety.
The Twelve Steps for me
are a safe place to recover.
Others like me come together
to support and encourage each other.
Together we are grateful
for what we have received,
for there we see at work
the hand of our Higher Power.
Prayer and meditation
are an important Step.
Prayer and meditation
bring us health and serenity.
I am grateful for my friends
who share my recovery.
Together we continue to pray
to sustain our daily sobriety.

PSALM 123

I lift my eyes
to you, Higher Power—
attentive to you
like a worker to a boss;
like the eyes of a slave
toward an owner,
I keep myself turned
toward you, my God.
Have pity on me, God,
for I've had my fill of contempt,
more than my share of ridicule
simply because I'm sick.

PSALM 124

"If God had not been with us,"
we addicts say,
"If God had not been with us
when our addictions overwhelmed us,
we would have been swallowed alive."
[We would have died by our own hands.]
Thanks be to you, God, who did not
allow our desires to destroy us.
We escaped with our lives
like a bear from a trap, like a bull
from the thrusts of a toreador.
Our help is found in a Higher Power,
a power greater than ourselves.

PSALM 125

We who trust in you, God,

are like Mount Everest—

steady and unwavering.

Our sobriety is rock solid,

founded firm on you alone,

one day at a time.

Our cravings will not overwhelm us.

Our abstinence must prevail through the day,

lest we turn once again to X and then fall.

God, grant safety to us in recovery,

to all of us who seek your healing.

Protect us from those still ensnared,

so we don't fall into those pits.

Peace to the Anonymous!

PSALM 126

When God set us free from bondage,

it seemed like a dream.

Then our hearts were filled with laughter

and our mouths burst forth in song.

Those who saw us were incredulous:

"God has worked a miracle," they said.

Oh yes, God worked a miracle for us

and we were astounded.

God, restore us from our enslavement;

bring us to life like water in a desert.

What began with our tears

will bear fruit in our joy.
We who walked away in despair
will come back with deep gratitude.
We will return to our daily lives
with a harvest of joyful freedom.

PSALM 127

If I don't rely on my Higher Power,
I struggle in vain for recovery.
If I don't turn my will over to God,
I cannot maintain my sobriety.
My promises will be broken;
my goals will not be attained.
My efforts will be wasted
because in this, only God can prevail.
Sobriety comes from a Higher Power;
recovery is an act of God.
My days of abstinence are gifts,
and nothing I deserve.
How blessed I am
as hours become days
and days become weeks.
I will not succumb
when temptation attacks.

PSALM 128

Blessed are we who trust in God,
who walk the Twelve-Step journey.

Fidelity to the Steps will bear fruit:

a new life becomes possible,

and the promises become real.

These good things come

to us who follow God's will.

We gain serenity and know peace,

and our fears diminish.

We will be blessed

when we trust in God.

God will bless us through our Program,

when we stay faithful to the Twelve Steps.

We will live and learn

and survive to see our descendants.

May recovery come to us all.

PSALM 129

We addicts can say,

"This disease has been around for a while.

It started when I was young,

but hasn't destroyed me yet.

It dug in and took root,

plowed deep tracks in my mind.

But God is good

and has whacked the deadly weeds."

May those who doubt the Program

find out better and return.

Let their fears soon wither up

like grass under the hot sun.

Let the harvest of their resentments
be tossed out as useless garbage,
so that others will see their sobriety
and bless God who has made them clean.

PSALM 130

In the depths of my despair
I cry out to you, God.
Please, hear my voice!
It's true that if you list my failures
then there's no way out of my shame.
But you are kind and merciful
and rescue me from my misery.
And so I wait for you, God;
I wait for some consolation.
My whole being waits impatiently
for a flicker of light in my darkness,
for some token of your forgiveness.
We addicts look to our Higher Power,
for there's still some hope with God,
God who rescues those who are lost.
Yes, God can save us weaklings
from all our afflictions.

PSALM 131

God, I avoid getting a big head
and keep myself focused on the "now."
I don't dwell on things

beyond my understanding.

I aim for peace and quiet myself

like a child in its parent's arms,

safe in an embrace of love.

I put my hope in you now

and for the rest of my life.

PSALM 132

God, will you please note in my favor

all the hardships I have endured?

Remember my sincere promises

to you, my Higher Power:

I admit that I'm powerless over X

and cannot manage my life;

I believe that you can restore me to sanity;

I turn over my will and my life to you;

I acknowledge my defects of character;

I'll make amends to those I have harmed;

I'll promptly admit when I'm wrong;

I'll seek your will and the power to carry it out;

and I'll practice these principles my whole life.

I heard about these things

and found out they are true.

In the process I found you,

and welcomed you into my life.

Let those who live these Steps

find their recovery in you;

Let those who are faithful to the Program

shout for joy in their healing.
You don't turn away from us,
and the Promises will come true:
we will find freedom and happiness,
and serenity will be ours.
We will manage our old regrets
and handle what comes each day.
For you will do for us
what we cannot do for ourselves.
Your mighty power comes
and works miracles in our lives.
We reach out to others who need help,
and together we make it.
We recover one day at a time,
and celebrate anniversaries.
You bring healing to those who are ill,
and restore the fallen with new life.
When we're recovering we prosper,
and so we keep coming back.

PSALM 133

How good it is
when addicts talk to each other;
for then we can make it together.
It's like cold water
poured on our heads
and down our backs
on a desert-hot day.

It's like fresh-fallen snow
frosting the mountains.
It is you, God,
refreshing our lives.

PSALM 134

Come together, all addicts;
show your gratitude to God today.
Give thanks to our Higher Power
when the moon and stars fill the sky.
For we've been blessed
with sobriety.

PSALM 135

We praise you, Higher Power,
we praise you for all you've done for us.
We gather together in groups;
we speak of the goodness shown to us.
4 For you've given us strength for abstinence,   — *being chosen*
granted us the gift of sobriety.
5 Your power is great,
beyond all other powers.
6 Whatever you set your mind to,
you can accomplish with ease,
to whomever and wherever you please—
conquer fears and heal resentments,
destroy dishonesty, remove self-centeredness.
Your mighty power stretched into our past;

you struck down what had seized us,
destroyed what enslaved us to X.
You loosed what had imprisoned us,
freed us from chains that had bound us.
You liberated us and gave us new life,
and we carry this message to others.
Your mighty power endures;
your healing strength lasts forever.
Again and again you prove it;
your desire is always to save us.
For we found things
and made them our gods;
they gave us words but not the truth;
they led to events but not reality;
they brought us relief but not serenity.
We paid dearly for what we sought,
but what we hoped for never came.
All you addicts, thank your God;
all dependents, your Higher Power!
All vulnerable people, thank your God;
all you powerless, your Higher Power!
May our Higher Power help us,
help us who follow the Steps.
Thank you, God!

PSALM 136

We thank you, God, who are always good,
>   for your healing lasts forever.
We thank you, Higher Power,
>   whose healing lasts forever.
We thank you, gracious God,
>   whose healing lasts forever;
who accomplishes marvelous deeds,
>   your healing lasts forever;
who made galaxies to fill the universe,
>   your healing lasts forever;
who made planets and gave us the earth,
>   your healing lasts forever;
who made sun and moon for day and night,
>   your healing lasts forever;
who sets us free from our slavery,
>   your healing lasts forever;
who liberates us from our bondage,
>   your healing lasts forever;
who guides us on a safe path,
>   your healing lasts forever;
who directs us from our distractions,
>   your healing lasts forever;
who steers us through the wilderness,
>   your healing lasts forever;
who conquers what seeks to destroy us,
>   your healing lasts forever;

who looses the chains that bind us,
>   your healing lasts forever;
who frees us from our prisons,
>   your healing lasts forever;
who gives us new life,
>   for your healing lasts forever.
You are mindful of human frailty,
>   and your healing lasts forever;
you rescue us from all dangers,
>   and your healing lasts forever;
you give us all we need,
>   and your healing lasts forever.
Give thanks to the Almighty,
>   for your healing lasts forever.

PSALM 137

When we were alone and lost,
we sat down and wept;
we remembered how life used to be.
There was no music left in us,
and when taunted,
we had no voice for singing,
no song of joy from our past.
How could we sing
when we were so sick?
How could I forget
what I had learned?
How could I lose

my hard-gained abstinence?

How could I stop working the Steps

that had kept my recovery alive?

I see my life

falling apart around me.

Destruction on every side,

I'm as bad off as I've ever been.

X dominates my life;

I am powerless over X.

I pray one day soon God will save me,

and crush the strong grip X has on me.

PSALM 138

I give thanks to you, Higher Power;

I am grateful with all my heart.

I give thanks in body and mind

for your healing strength in my life,

for your power is greater than all else.

When I asked, you answered me,

and granted me recovery.

All who are abstinent give you thanks,

for they know your gentle strength.

They tell others the saving message

that rescued their life from destruction.

There are none too high or low

whom you are powerless to save.

Even when I walk on the edge of a cliff,

you can save me from a great fall.

You provide the words of life,

and speak the truth to my heart.

You have a purpose for my life;

your healing lasts forever.

Don't forget now the one you have saved.

PSALM 139

My God, you have scrutinized me thoroughly;

you know my thoughts better than I do;

whether I'm close or far off, you know me well.

You know the direction I'm headed

and where it will take me.

Even before I open my mouth

you know what I'm going to say.

And yet you enfold me,

and lay a protective hand upon me.

It's too much for me to take in;

I can hardly absorb the wonder of it.

Is there any place I can disappear?

Any place where you can't find me?

If I fly to the clouds, you are there;

If I flee to a cave, you are there;

East or west, north or south,

you encompass me with your care

and keep me safe and sound.

If I think, "I'll hide in the dark,"

you still know where I am.

There is no place I can go

that hides me from your loving sight.
You are the one who created me,
who knows me through and through.
I thank you for my existence,
for making me awesome and wonderful.
Your works are amazing, that I know.
Since the moment I was conceived
you've known my body well;
from that time forward you've seen my path
and you know how my life will evolve.
The awareness of this overwhelms me;
it's too much for my mind to handle.
Your immensity is beyond my grasp;
and yet, when I die, you'll be with me.
So I ask for your divine protection
from this disease that seeks my life,
from the thoughts that cloud my reason,
from the behavior that drags me down.
Can you see that I'm trying,
striving to change my thinking,
and struggling to change my behavior?
Sometimes I hate myself;
I hate what I've become.
God, look into my heart and see my true desire.
Help me to know your will and do it,
and toss out every obstacle that hinders me;
lead me on the Twelve-Step path to recovery.

PSALM 140

1 Free me, God from this madness;   *— evil men*

  save me from my addiction, *— violent men*

2-5 2 from thinking that's messed up my life,

  and lies that have caused me to fail.

3 Rescue me, God, from the clutches of this disease,

  save me from the illness that's killing me,

  for powerful feelings grab me

  and strong emotions attack my heart.

6 I turn to you, God, and say:

  "You are my Higher Power;

  listen to my prayer.

7 God, you're my mighty strength

  who protects me in battle against X;

  God addiction — txt: you have covered my head in battle

8 don't let my addiction conquer me.

  — "grant the desires of the wicked"

  There are people around me who expect me to fail;

  may their own doubts be their downfall.

  Let their misery and their failures

  cause them to collapse (just like they expect of me).

  May our harsh judgments of one another cease

  before we all end up destroyed.

  For I know, God, that you can save us:

  you will raise the fallen and addicted.

  Then we'll thank you for deliverance,

  and praise your mighty power.

PSALM 141

1 God, I call to you, I need you NOW!
  Listen closely; I need your help!
2 May my words rise to you like incense;
  my hands raised in prayer reach toward you.
3 Put an angel at the door of my lips;
  safeguard what goes into my mouth.
4 Don't let my mind be attracted to X, — *any evil thing*
  nor turn to things that drag me down;
  Don't allow me to join the addicted
  who tell me that everything's fine.
  Let those in recovery teach me,
  and those in my group correct me.
  Don't let crazy thinking corrupt me,
  because my desire is to do your will.
  If I fall off the wagon, save me,
  so I learn your wisdom once more,
  lest I end up with broken bones
  shattered in a fall from a cliff.
  I turn to you once more, my God;
  don't desert me or leave me defenseless.
  Protect me from what makes me stumble,
  from the traps that ensnare and kill me.
  Even though others may fall,
  protect me so I don't crash and burn.

PSALM 142

I cry out to my Higher Power;
I raise my voice so you can hear my plea.
I complain about my life,
and tell you my troubles.
Even when I'm falling,
you know where I'm headed.
As I try to walk the Twelve Steps
I still fall into traps—
I look around and it seems
that "no one notices me;"
"there is no place that's safe;"
and "no one cares about me."
I shout to you, God:
"You are my saving Power,
the one who can save my life."
Save me from my addictions
because they are too strong for me.
Rescue me from this prison
and I'll always be grateful to you.
The abstinent will gather with me
and together we will recover.

PSALM 143

O God, hear my prayer.
Listen carefully for I'm in great need;
answer me as only you can do.
Do not judge me, please,

for no one can measure up to you.
My addiction has chased me down
and worn me out;
I live in darkness as though I'm dead.
My inner spirit sighs within me;
my mind is disgusted by my behavior.
I can remember days gone by.
I reflect upon your goodness
and the wonderful things you did.
Now I reach out to you
and my guts thirst for you
like a land long in drought.
Answer me soon, my God,
because I'm failing fast.
Don't hide from me now
or I'll not raise my head again.
Remind me of your faithful love
so that I can place my trust in you.
Show me the path to follow
as I promise to follow your will.
Save me, God, from my disease;
I come to you seeking safety.
Teach me to do your will
because you are God,
and you know best
where to lead me.
You are the Higher Power
who can save my life.

Your powerful wisdom

can save me from myself.

In your great strength vanquish this disease;

destroy my addiction, as I follow the Steps.

PSALM 144

You are strong, my God, my rock,

who train my thoughts for recovery,

who are my strength and my right mind,

my might and my straight thinking,

my protector who saves me from nonsense,

who defeats my stinkin' thinkin'.

Who are we, mere mortals,

to think that we are wise?

Our ideas are no more than sparks;

the flash of a thought can vanish.

Higher Power, leave your heavens,

and come to heal our minds.

Send your wisdom to replace our insanity,

good judgment to heal our craziness.

Good God, come to me—

rescue me from stupidity,

save me from impulsivity,

free me from my deceptions,

and help me to recognize your truth.

I'll sing out to you with gratitude

and make music to please my God,

who rescues the higher-ups,

and liberates the lowly.

Higher Power, help me!

Guide my thinking, my God!

Deliver me from clever thoughts

that lead to my own destruction.

We pray for our sons and daughters,

that they mature into healthy adults.

May our cupboards be filled,

and our crops be bounteous;

our flocks increase tenfold,

and our herds a hundredfold.

May our cities be without violence,

and the countryside be safe for all.

We are privileged who receive these blessings;

we are fortunate to be familiar with God's works.

PSALM 145

I am grateful to you, my God,

and will praise your power forever.

I will acclaim you each day

and will thank you every day of my life.

Those in Program tell one another

about the good things you have done for us.

I will remember your power,

and speak of your wonderous works.

I will proclaim your awesome might,

and declare the goodness shown me.

We shall celebrate the fame of your healing

and shout the news of our recovery.
You are compassion and love,
slow to anger, and rich in kindness.
You offer your love to all people,
and your compassion fills the cosmos.
All of creation owes you thanks,
and all people should be grateful.
We should speak of the vast universe
and the energy of your creation,
so that all people know of your power
and how you extend yourself to us.
Your creation is an everlasting reign,
a sovereignty that will last forever.
You are faithful to your promises,
and generous in all your deeds.
You lift up those who have fallen,
and gather those who've been cast aside.
All those in need wait for you,
and you grant our needs when the time is right.
You open yourself in love
and satisfy our deepest desires.
Your ways are just,
and your deeds are merciful.
You hear our lonely cries
when we reach out to you in our need.
When we accept your will to save us,
you rescue us with your healing power.
You watch over us with love,

and mourn the loss of the addicted.

I will praise you, my Higher Power,

and proclaim your goodness forever.

PSALM 146

I praise you, God, with my whole being.

I am grateful every day of my life,

and will never cease to thank you.

I don't put my trust in X,

it has no power to save me.

It lasts for a while, then fades away,

and what it claims to offer never lasts.

Blessed are we who find our help in you;

you are my hope and my healing.

My help comes from a Higher Power,

a Power greater than myself, always faithful.

You bring sobriety to the addicted,

and health to all who are ill.

You set captives free from their slavery,

and protect the downtrodden, hopeless, and lost.

Our Higher Power sets us free

from the prison of our disease;

and helps us to see the error of our ways.

You pull upright those who have fallen,

and love the new life we have found.

You save us from insanity,

help us to see the truth of things,

and save us from stinkin' thinkin'.

Our Higher Power will always be around,

there's no day when you are not present.

Thank you, God!

PSALM 147

Praise God!

It feels great to praise you

who have been so good to me;

praise is just so right.

You build up our Twelve-Step programs;

you gather us outcasts together.

You heal our brokenness

and bind up our wounds.

Despite our huge number,

you know us each by name.

Great are you, my God,

an awesome Higher Power,

whose depth of understanding

takes my breath away.

You lift up those who have fallen,

and bring down those who shun you.

I sing out to you with gratitude,

and make music to please my Power.

You spill rain from the heavens

and till the soil of my heart

to bring forth a great harvest.

All creatures receive from your bounty;

your generous love is poured out to all.

You are not impressed by *my* strength,

and find no delight in *my* power.

Rather, you find pleasure in my efforts,

in people who put trust in you.

All addicts: praise God,

praise our Higher Power!

For you strengthen us constantly,

and send us grace as we need it.

You grant peace to our minds,

and fill us with serenity.

You know the words to speak

that make us calm again.

You share your gifts generously,

like abundant rain and snow falling to earth.

Whose generosity can match yours?

You offer us words of wisdom,

and speak to us with encouragement—

who understands us like you do?

You give us the wisdom of Twelve Steps

to guide us from despair to hope.

No one else can save us; for they

don't really understand our addictions.

Thank you, God!

PSALM 148

Praise God!

Praise God in the heavens;

Praise God on the earth below.

Praise God, all spiritual beings,

and all who are human, praise God.

Praise God, sun and moon;

Praise God, stars that shine.

Praise God, Milky Way,

and galaxies that fill the sky.

Let everything praise you,

for you are the Creator of all—

who brought forth the dry land

and set the limits of the seas.

Let all creatures praise you,

who made all that swim in the seas.

Fire and hail, snow and frost—

all proceed from your hand—

mountains and hills,

fruit trees and redwoods,

wild animals and house pets,

all creatures great and small;

citizens and politicians,

elected and volunteers,

the young and the old,

men and women alike.

Let everyone praise you, God,

who does what no one else can,

whose strength now fills the land.

You have restored our honor;

we have reason to praise you still—

the people who call on you for help,

who strive to follow your will.

Praise God!

PSALM 149

Praise God!

Raise your voice in a new song;

join those who rejoice in recovery.

Let addicts rejoice in their Higher Power;

let all addicts rejoice in their God.

Praise God with joyful dancing

and jubilant music through the night.

For you take delight in all people

and have given the humble a victory.

Let the sober be filled with gratitude

and be thankful through the day and night too!

Let our voices be filled with praise,

the song of victory fill our throats.

Let the oppressed know there is hope,

that their lives can be raised from the dust.

Their addictions can be conquered

by a Higher Power's might,

taken from them and beaten.

The power of God can do this!

Praise God!

PSALM 150

Praise God!

Praise our cosmic God

whose presence fills the universe!

Praise God for wonderful works;

praise God for healing might.

Praise God with blast of brass;

praise God with sonorous strings.

Praise God with blowing winds;

praise God with pounding percussion.

Let the galaxies and what fills them

praise our Higher Power!

Praise God!

The Twelve Steps

1. We admitted we were powerless over . . . —that our lives had become unmanageable.

2. Came to believe that a Power greater than ourselves could restore us to sanity.

3. Made a decision to turn our will and our lives over to the care of God *as we understood Him.*

4. Made a searching and fearless moral inventory of ourselves.

5. Admitted to God, to ourselves, and to another human being the exact nature of our wrongs.

6. Were entirely ready to have God remove all these defects of character.

7. Humbly asked Him to remove our shortcomings.

8. Made a list of all persons we had harmed, and became willing to make amends to them all.

9. Made direct amends to such people wherever possible, except when to do so would injure them or others.

10. Continued to take personal inventory and when we were wrong promptly admitted it.

11. Sought through prayer and meditation to improve our conscious contact with God, *as we understood Him,* praying only for knowledge of His will for us and the power to carry that out.

12. Having had a spiritual awakening as the result of these Steps, we tried to carry this message to . . ., and to practice these principles in all our affairs.

The Twelve Steps of Alcoholics Anonymous are adapted with permission of Alcoholics Anonymous World Services, Inc. ("AAWS") Permission to adapt the Twelve Steps does not mean that AAWS has reviewed or approved the contents of this publication, or that AAWS necessarily agrees with the views expressed herein. A.A. is a program of recovery from alcoholism only - use of the Twelve Steps in connection with programs and activities which are patterned after A.A., but which address other problems, or in any other non-A.A. context, does not imply otherwise. Additionally, while A.A. is a spiritual program, A.A. is not a religious program. Thus, A.A. is not affiliated or allied with any sect, denomination, or specific religious belief.

Index

205